What Do We Do When Nobody Is Listening?

What Do We Do When Nobody Is Listening?

*Leading the Church in
a Polarized Society*

Robin W. Lovin

WILLIAM B. EERDMANS PUBLISHING COMPANY
GRAND RAPIDS, MICHIGAN

Wm. B. Eerdmans Publishing Co.
4035 Park East Court SE, Grand Rapids, Michigan 49546
www.eerdmans.com

Published 2022
Printed in the United States of America

28 27 26 25 24 23 22   1 2 3 4 5 6 7

ISBN 978-0-8028-8232-5

Library of Congress Cataloging-in-Publication Data

A catalog record for this book is available from the Library of
    Congress.

But to what will I compare this generation? It is like children sitting in the marketplaces and calling to one another,

> "We played the flute for you, and you did
>   not dance;
> we wailed, and you did not mourn."

For John came neither eating or drinking, and they say, "He has a demon"; the Son of Man came eating and drinking, and they say, "Look, a glutton and a drunkard, a friend of tax collectors and sinners!" Yet wisdom is vindicated by her deeds.

—Matthew 11:16–19 NRSV

Contents

Foreword

In this excellent book, Professor Lovin asks of churches, pastors, and leaders, What do we do when nobody is listening? He recognizes that the church and people of faith may have an important role to play in our fractured society, but that society no longer seems to pay attention. To this question he offers a thoughtful response that includes a pathway forward that is crucial if the church is to be part of the solution, rather than the problem, in our hyperpolarized world.

While the broader society may not be listening, those people in our pews who are still showing up often *are* listening, but they sometimes hear through the filter of their political or sociological convictions, convictions often shaped less by the Word than by Fox or CNN, Facebook or Twitter, or their favorite podcaster.

This week I received a message from a woman angry that I had agreed to be interviewed by the leader of a conservative think tank. I saw it as a bridge-building opportunity and a chance to share my perspectives on inclusion. She was incensed that I would speak at this organization that she viewed with disdain. She noted that my "conservative" leanings were obvious, and then she said, "I will never listen to another word you ever say. Your words mean nothing to me."

On that same day, I received an email from a man in my congregation who wrote that my "liberal" views, particularly on racial justice, have left him disappointed and for that reason he is reducing his pledge to the church. He wrote that it was clear to him that I listen to the liberals but not to the conservatives in our congregation.

This is where many pastors and church leaders live today, caught between the two "sides" and suspect by members of each. Mainline churches are among the few places where we might still find people on the left and right in the same room focused on common goals. But pastors often find it difficult to navigate the increasingly turbulent waters of issues that divide their members, and hence some have resorted to keeping their head down and not touching on anything that is remotely divisive—a near impossibility today as nearly everything has become politicized.

"Liberal" and "conservative" are both good words. To be liberal is to be generous and open to seeing things in new ways—open to reform. To be conservative is to be grounded and to carefully conserve that which must be conserved. Ideally, we're all liberal conservatives or conservative liberals. This valuing of both sides of this equation and a willingness to hold on to both impulses is what helps us find balance and to find a path forward through our divisions. But doing this is hard work.

One bishop recently told me that a third of the pastors serving under his leadership had retired in the last couple of years. Most were simply tired of the conflict. He noted that local churches had become markedly less gracious toward their pastors in the last two years.

At a recent conference hosted by the Church of the Resurrection, several hundred pastors of leading churches and young clergy were surveyed to find out how they are feeling after serving their churches through a pandemic, the debates about masks and vaccines, a divisive political season, marches for racial justice, and denominational conflicts over human sexuality. Surprisingly, their top answer was "hopeful." But not far behind were "exhausted" and "anxious."

The hopefulness of these seven hundred pastors and church leaders we surveyed came, in part, from the recognition that the church may be the best surviving hope for addressing their brokenness in our society.

It is easy for the church's gospel to be distorted by the influence of the world. And at times preachers and church leaders, when they do screw up the courage to speak on difficult issues, do so in a way that only adds to the polarization. Among the questions church leaders must ask when they are speaking to divisive issues is, Is my goal merely to irritate my hearers, or is it to influence them?

Irritating people is easy and requires no real skill as an orator. But influencing them requires listening to your hearers and finding ways to speak to them that invite them to see things differently from how they had before.

In their recent book *The Upswing: How America Came Together a Century Ago and How We Can Do It Again*, Robert Putnam, Malkin Research Professor of Public Policy at Harvard's Kennedy School, and coauthor Shaylyn Romney Garrett note that society at the end of the nineteenth century was, like today, deeply divided. Among the critical factors in healing the divide in the first half of the twentieth century was the church with its union of a deeply personal faith with a concern for the common good—what some would call the union of the evangelical and social gospels.

This is the hope I hear in the book you now hold. Professor Lovin writes as a scholar, but his proposal is intensely pastoral. He invites us to reclaim a church that carries *gravitas*—gravity—which he speaks of as "taking up space." He calls us to listen, first to the Word of God and then to one another and finally to those whose voices are seldom heard. Listening is nearly a lost art in our divided times. But listening is part of the answer to healing our world.

I've found that when I meet with people who are upset with something I've said, or the church has said, and we sit down and talk together, we nearly always end up reconciled, even if we disagree. The conversations start with seeking to convey my love for the person and my appreciation for them, which opens the door both for my listening to them and their listening to me. We often both find we've misunderstood the other.

I was reminded as I read Professor Lovin's words about formation that our souls, and the souls of all within the church (and in the world), are constantly being formed, in large part by the voices they are listening to. Paul's words in Romans 12:2 are particularly instructive: "Don't be conformed to the patterns of this world, but be transformed by the renewing of your minds so that you can figure out what God's will is—what is good and pleasing and mature."

Ultimately, Professor Lovin's proposal addresses not only the church's ability to speak in a way that an unlistening world might hear a Word that can heal it but also its ability to speak to a listening church that may have lost its saltiness, and whose light is dimmed by its own divisions.

Several times throughout this important book, Robin Lovin mentions the idea that the divisions we experience today are captured on the T-shirts of people on either side of the dividing line. During the pandemic, after a summer of racial protests, while people were fighting over masks, and just before the most divisive election in decades, our congregation launched a campaign in Kansas City aimed at depolarizing our community. We were seeking to "take up space." The campaign was simple. It included campaign signs placed on every street corner next to the signs of candidates. It included sermons and Bible studies. It included thirty days of kindness lived out by our members. And yes, like every good campaign, it included T-shirts. The signs and T-shirts carried one simple message, #loveyourneighbor.

The church may be the last, best hope for healing our divided society. Professor Lovin offers a roadmap for how we might do just that.

ADAM HAMILTON
Senior Pastor, The United Methodist
Church of the Resurrection
Leawood, Kansas

$$\left[\begin{array}{c} \textrm{PART I} \\ \textit{Divisions} \end{array}\right]$$

We live in a divided society. We are a people with many different backgrounds and interests. Through our different experiences, we come to value different things, and we end up working toward different goals. As a result, we often differ about how to educate our children, how to provide access to health care, and how to balance individual and social responsibilities for employment, housing, and the needs of everyday life.

Disagreements like these are inevitable in a democracy, especially one that spreads across a wide territory and incorporates varied cultures, traditions, and ways of life. The authors of the United States Constitution recognized this and tried to design a political system that could facilitate compromises and accommodate enduring differences. But at times of crisis, divisions run deep and sometimes, they reach the breaking point. That happened in the crisis leading up to the Civil War, as different ideas about slavery, democracy, and national unity that had been argued for decades could no longer be held together. In a similar way, the beginning of the Great Depression marked a crisis provoked not only by economic collapse, but by radically different ideas about how to deal with it. Deep disagreements like these mark points of decision and realignments of political forces that change the future.

Many worry that we are approaching another such crisis in these first decades of the twenty-first century. Since the end of the Second World War, we have disagreed with one another about civil rights, economic opportunity, and America's place in the world. But in recent years, the disagreements have become so sharp that we seem to be drawn up in opposing sides that stare at each other across an empty space without shared purposes or values— perhaps even without shared facts.

But if this is a crisis, it is oddly unlike those earlier ones that shaped our history. No one great issue divides us, and no specific set of events drove us into our opposing camps. The pandemic of 2020 and the sharp economic downturn that accompanied it provided focus for our discontents, but the national divide over public health measures, economic policy, and civil unrest seemed less a matter of crisis response and more like two sides that were already lined up against one another, calculating how to incorporate unexpected events into a narrative they had already rehearsed. The language was sometimes apocalyptic, but beneath the rhetoric of an uncivil presidential campaign and a closely divided election, events flowed in familiar channels. Many of us worried about the aftermath of the election and predicted worse things to come, but few really expected anything different.

Instead of reaching a crisis point of unsustainable disagreement, our political parties, regions, social classes, ethnic groups, and attitudes have assembled themselves over the decades into two broad though barely coherent coalitions. Political scientists and policy analysts identify this phenomenon as "polarization" or "political sectarianism."* Like feuding religious groups or partisan ideologues, these "sects" continue to assert their claims to truth whether or not anyone is listening, so that our public discourse now seems devoted to energizing the faithful and to recruiting the diminishing number of unaligned people in the middle into one base or the other—red states and blue states, working class or professional elite, globalists and patriots. This does not quite live up to our civics textbook picture of politics, but if it is a crisis, it is a remarkably stable one, with each side dependent on the other for its identity and agenda. We are a divided society. Our candidates, elected officials, political strategists, and media specialists have simply adapted to this reality, with varying degrees of success.

* Eli J. Finkel et al., "Political Sectarianism in America," *Science* 370, no. 6516 (October 30, 2020): 533-36.

Churches, too, have adapted to this polarization, and sometimes they have led the way into it. They have moved away from parishes and congregations built around local communities. They have sorted their membership along lines that reflect economic and cultural groups in the wider society. When the tensions within congregations and denominations became too much to continue together, they split up. A divided society also divides our congregations, denominations, and the way we see other people of faith. If Christianity itself is not to be redefined in polarized terms, we must rediscover how the gospel teaches us to understand ourselves, our neighbors, and the purposes of politics.

The first step, part 1 of this book, is to get an overview of the situation in which we find ourselves. We will see how polarization developed over recent decades and how, despite all the conflicts and dysfunctions, we have adapted to a divided society (chapter 1). Next, we review how churches, in particular, have adapted to social changes and sometimes tried to resist them (chapter 2). The dysfunctions of polarization in church and society lead, in turn, to part 2, which considers how Christians might shape a different response by listening to the Word of God (chapter 3), to the world (chapter 4), and to those who have not been heard (chapter 5). What we learn at each step will change the way we see the big problems, but the real test will be how these ways of listening reshape our congregations, vocations, and communities.

Polarization

Disagreement is inevitable in a modern, pluralistic society. People are shaped by different experiences, and they bring different needs and aspirations to places where they work together with others from different backgrounds. They share neighborhoods with people from different cultures, and sometimes they struggle just to move down the street together without getting too much in one another's way. The COVID-19 pandemic reminded us that "social distance" is something that is hard to achieve without constant negotiations. People differ about the details of everyday life and also about the big ideas that determine what they want for themselves and their families and what they expect from others who dream and plan alongside them. Moreover, our different desires and expectations are not just a checklist we consult when we have a decision to make. We form our identity around them, so that our differences are always with us. We belong to an ethnic group. We have a certain kind of job and the life expectations that go with it. We have a family and a faith, whether or not these look like what other people expect a family or a faith to be. Our identity determines how others see us, and thus it becomes the way we see ourselves, too. These differences in background and experience and the identities we develop through them mark out potential disagreements, as different identities give rise to different interests.

The structures of modern life create other tensions within institutions between management and workers, or between "shareholders" and "stakeholders." Other disagreements characteristically mark the relations between different kinds of institutions, as for-profit corporations, academic institutions, social service agencies, and community organizations vie for support, customers, clients, or favorable legislation. Still other conflicts arise from the different interests of urban and rural communities or from conditions that separate different regions of the country. It was not for nothing that the framers of our Constitution worried about whether its republican form of government could encompass so large and diverse a geographic area.

Reasonable Pluralism

Given the scope of today's conflicts, it is important to remember that over the course of our history, we have usually been able to arrive at some working agreements, and even as the differences persist, we create systems and procedures designed to moderate our conflicts, rather than intensify them. Such interim answers are characteristic of life in a modern democracy, and troubling as our conflicts may be, it would be more worrisome if the disagreements disappeared—if they were forced underground by an authoritarian regime, or if a wave of populist enthusiasm silenced those who still felt marginalized and excluded. Partial answers and temporary fixes are the main political products of a modern democracy, even for those who keep hoping and working for justice, compassion, and equal opportunity. As Reinhold Niebuhr put it, democracy is "a method of finding proximate solutions for insoluble problems."*

For those who have a deep faith in the ideals of justice and equality, the compromises are frustrating, but learning to live with them is one of the conditions of what the philosopher John Rawls calls "reasonable pluralism."** A modern democracy will have some ongoing disagreements in its public life as long as it continues to exist as a democracy. Reasonable people accept this necessity and operate within the conditions.

Reasonable pluralism, however, is not an easy achievement, and there are moments that stretch its conditions to the breaking point. Sometimes an attempt at democracy fails at the outset. The United States Constitution barely survived the struggle for its ratification, as regions differed over the public role of religion, over the proposed federal government's powers of taxation, and especially over slav-

---

* Reinhold Niebuhr, *The Children of Light and the Children of Darkness: A Vindication of Democracy and a Critique of Its Conventional Defense* (New York: Charles Scribner's Sons, 1960), 118.

** John Rawls, *Political Liberalism* (New York: Columbia University Press, 1993), 36–38.

ery.* The working arrangements that papered over the disagreement about slavery eventually broke down as a cotton economy built on slave labor grew and pressure mounted for its expansion into new territories in the West. It took a civil war to amend the constitutional arrangements, but the decades that followed the Reconstruction Amendments gave rise to a system of legal segregation that lasted nearly a century. Its effects persist in structures that divide opportunities and outcomes along racial lines today. Especially around issues of race, then, American democracy lives with the uneasy knowledge that disagreements held together by reasonable pluralism can give way to more intense conflicts that threaten dissolution.

The unavoidable question, after two decades of congressional gridlock, periodic government shutdowns, contested election results, and increasing urban unrest, is whether we have now come to one of those points where the politics of reasonable pluralism come up short and conflict escalates toward dissolution. To offer a word of reassurance at the outset, the idea I want to put forward in this book is that we are not *yet* at such point of crisis. But neither is the polarization we experience today simply a continuation of the usual politics of disagreement. The divisions run through our whole society, not just our politics. Our churches, neighborhoods, and universities are discovering that they live along the fault lines between progressive and conservative, just like our legislatures and political leaders. Pastors, professors, CEOs, and directors of human resources learn to adapt, along with the

---

* Pauline Meier, *Ratification* (New York: Simon & Schuster, 2010).

senators and representatives. Some, in fact, turn the divisions quite successfully to their own advantage.

For that reason, the structures of polarization turn out to be surprisingly stable. Ours is neither a time of ordinary politics nor a moment of extraordinary crisis. This is something different, and it could continue for a long time. But before we settle into this "new normal," we need to ask whether we are making use of the situation, or whether the situation is using us. In most cases, I think, the answer is that the situation is using us. Precisely because politics has adapted so successfully to its requirements, it is going to take some new ways of thinking in other institutions and communities to avoid embedding these divisions in our society for the long run.

What that might mean becomes starkly apparent when an emergency such the COVID-19 pandemic or an upsurge in police violence against people of color draws our attention to another kind of polarization. Set alongside the division into red states and blue states that is hollowing out the middle of our politics, we see the hollowing out of society as a whole, a widening gap between those for whom wealth and opportunities are increasing and a larger group for whom they are actually shrinking. In popular wisdom, death and illness are the great equalizers, putting rich and poor, powerful and weak all on the same footing. But it turns out that in the society we are creating for ourselves, death and illness fall disproportionately on the poor and weak. Political polarization alone does not *cause* this polarization of possibilities, but it is making it impossible for us to deal with it, and that sets us up for a real crisis which our busy adaptations to a divided society will not be able to prevent.

Disagreement and Social Transformation

To see what is different about the present disagreements, it is helpful to review how we arrived at this point. This is not a matter of specialized historical research. The main events are well known. But if we look back on them from where we are now, they may appear differently from the ways they appear in our history books or the ways we experienced them at the time.

If we look for transformative moments in American history, it is not necessary to go back to the Civil War or the ratification of the Constitution. The Great Depression that began in 1929 was marked by widespread failure of economic and political systems, and the sense of crisis was intensified by similar failures elsewhere around the world. The First World War had toppled European empires, destroyed their economies, and launched the resentments that would bring nationalist regimes to power in Japan, Italy, and Germany. After a Russian revolution that overthrew the czar, Lenin's Bolsheviks seized power and established the Soviet Union. Set against that background, talk of a possible revolution in the United States was not mere rhetoric or political fiction, though there was plenty of both of those.* Christian social teaching responded to the moment in the work of Dorothy Day (1897–1980), John A. Ryan (1869–1945), and Reinhold Niebuhr (1892–1971). For Protestants, especially, Niebuhr captured the moment with the publication of *Moral Man*

---

* Sinclair Lewis, *It Can't Happen Here* (Garden City, NY: Doubleday, 1936).

and Immoral Society in 1932. Here, the hope for a gradual transformation of society by Christian ideals gives way to a stark contrast between the attitudes of proletarian classes and the attitudes of privileged classes and a warning that the privileged will not give up their power unless they are forced to do so.*

Reinhold Niebuhr's "Christian realism" would dominate social ethics in America for the next three decades, but the realistic assessment of the privileged and the proletarians would be replaced by an ironic view of global conflict between the idealistic "children of light" and the self-interested "children of darkness."** For a Niebuhrian realist, of course, the children of light are never as pure as they think themselves to be, but their democratic commitments offered the best possibility for containing the totalitarianism that results when self-interest is pursued to its inevitable conclusion. The conflict between the two forces is real, and it mirrors in some respects the opposition in *Moral Man and Immoral Society*, but during the Second World War and the long Cold War that followed, this global conflict helped the United States

---

* Reinhold Niebuhr, *Moral Man and Immoral Society* (Louisville: Westminster John Knox, 2001); Harlan Beckley, *Passion for Justice: Retrieving the Legacies of Walter Rauschenbusch, John A. Ryan, and Reinhold Niebuhr* (Louisville: Westminster John Knox, 1992); John Laughery and Blythe Randolph, *Dorothy Day: Dissenting Voice of the American Century* (New York: Simon & Schuster, 2020); Christine Firer Hinze, *Radical Sufficiency: Work, Livelihood, and a U.S. Catholic Economic Ethic* (Washington, DC: Georgetown University Press, 2021).

** Reinhold Niebuhr, *The Irony of American History* (New York: Charles Scribner's Sons, 1952).

to maintain domestic political tranquility. It put a premium on symbolism that united us and downplayed the rhetoric of our deepest divisions, whether these were regional, racial, religious, or economic. This was the era of patriotism and the "Judeo-Christian" heritage.* Even the grim realities of segregation could be covered by the expectation that the nation that was committed to secure human freedom globally would eventually have to make good on that promise for its own people.**

Well before the end of the Cold War, however, deeper tensions in the democratic ideal resurfaced in mass movements directed toward ending racial segregation, poverty, gender discrimination, and other injustices. From the early 1950s, a strategy of litigation designed to make the constitutional requirement of equal citizenship real in practice began to dismantle segregation in political practices and, importantly, in public education. That legal effort led by Thurgood Marshall resulted in the Supreme Court's 1954 decision in *Brown v. Board of Education*, which ruled against legal segregation in public education and paved the way for federal intervention where required to end it. Changes won in the courts coincided with changes brought about by local efforts to desegregate public transportation and other services. The Montgomery Bus Boycott (1955–56) pioneered the

---

* K. Healan Gaston, *Imagining Judeo-Christian America: Religion, Secularism, and the Redefinition of Democracy* (Chicago: University of Chicago Press, 2019).

** Gunnar Myrdal, *An American Dilemma* (New York: Harper & Bros., 1944).

model of a disciplined grassroots movement for change. Martin Luther King Jr. crafted a theology and a strategy for the movement that spread rapidly across the South, and expanded to include legislative goals, including voting rights laws and equal access to housing. In the 1960s, the movement made its appearance in Northern cities where discrimination was no less pervasive.*

The strategy of mass protest and nonviolent resistance stretched democracy's methods for handling disagreement to their limits, but it proved Niebuhr and other realists wrong when they worried that change was coming too fast and would provoke massive resistance that could undo what had been gained. One important reason for this success was the ability of King and his movement to build coalitions and make connections across a range of issues, resulting in a more comprehensive ideal of social justice. Part of the strategy of nonviolent protest was to meet the opposition in their humanity and to show them their human bond with those they were trying to dominate and exclude. King also easily accepted other groups with other agendas, so that the movement came to include poverty and peace, as well as racial equality, in its primary goals. These could easily have been seen as political competitors, but for a time, at least, they literally marched arm in arm. The Civil Rights Movement aroused resistance, raised tensions, and sometimes provoked a violent response; but its approach to its opponents, rivals,

---

* Martin Luther King Jr., *Stride toward Freedom: The Montgomery Story* (New York: Harper & Row, 1958); *Where Do We Go from Here: Chaos or Community?* (New York: Harper & Row, 1967).

and hesitant allies was the opposite of the polarizing strategies that dominate our public life today.

Like Gandhi's nonviolent movement that was one of its inspirations, the Civil Rights Movement in the United States has become a sign of hope well beyond the place where it began. Its example is invoked everywhere that entrenched discrimination, authoritarian rulers, and ethnic rivalries are challenged by popular resistance. It is an inspiration to the oppressed everywhere and a warning to leaders who bet their continuation in power on repression. But if its effects around the world have proved far more extensive and durable than worried realists feared at the beginning, the results still fall short of idealist hope, especially in the United States where the dream began.

From Transformation to Fragmentation

In part, that is because the strategies that launched the social transformation in the middle of the last century simply reached the limits of their effectiveness. Protest is effective in raising a range of issues, but not all of the problems that bring people into the streets can easily be formulated into specific policy goals. Obtaining voting rights for disenfranchised African Americans in the South could be attached to a specific piece of legislation that became the Voting Rights Act of 1965. But if the vote did not by itself secure expanded opportunities, what then? And what about demands for workplace equality, or recognition of new forms of family life, or expanded opportunities for people with different abilities, or any of a myriad of other aspirations that could not be simply translated into straightforward political measures or specific laws?

In addition, the very success of the Civil Rights Movement led others to adopt its strategies for different, even opposed, goals. And unlike the coalition for justice that shows up at the Lincoln Memorial to commemorate the March on Washington, some of the newer movements are not so good at building alliances that could encompass policy commitments across a range of different issues. "Single issue politics" with a focus on race, abortion, gender equality, or religious freedom emerged to challenge both older models of political compromise and the broadly based activist groups that grew out of the Civil Rights Movement. As the movement organizations of the 1960s and 1970s settled into their own place in the political establishment and their leaders took well-deserved places in Congress, statehouses, and city councils, the new trajectory of politics moved from coalition toward fragmentation, with a growing number of interest groups prepared to make their single issue the touchstone of political loyalty and perhaps of moral legitimacy, too.*

It was during these years that mainstream Protestantism, which gave broad support to the civil rights coalition, experienced a resurgence of fundamentalism, and several denominations split over theological and moral issues. Conservative Catholics began to question the changes that began with the Second Vatican Council and

---

* Daniel T. Rogers, *The Age of Fracture* (Cambridge, MA: Belknap Press of Harvard University Press, 2011).

the social activism associated with Liberation Theology. The 1980s was also the decade of Jerry Falwell's Moral Majority, which worked across a broad front that included both political and religious goals. What we would today identify as "progressive" politics also coalesced during these years, as well as the tendency to impose a kind of progressive orthodoxy that its opponents would label "political correctness."*

As political movements multiplied and fragmented, each generated its own orthodoxy that rejected other terms for framing the questions. Public discourse sometimes seemed to consist of little more than competing demands set out in competing moral vocabularies, without enough common ground even to make an argument possible. The aspirational biblical language of justice and peace could no longer provide symbolic unity, since people in the churches were sometimes using it against each other. With religious leaders divided among themselves and the symbols of civic unity that their traditions had provided increasingly contested, aspirations for justice were increasingly overshadowed by the fear that disagreement was becoming unmanageable.

The End of Reasonable Pluralism?

To provide new terms on which the public argument could continue, philosophers and historians turned to

---

* Allan Bloom, *The Closing of the American Mind* (New York: Simon & Schuster, 1987).

the practices of liberal democracy itself. It was for this purpose that John Rawls introduced the idea of "reasonable pluralism" that we mentioned earlier. The phrase was new, but it took its origin from much older ideas of reason and tolerance. A society that includes people with very different ideas about reality and about the lives they want for themselves must devise ways to make political decisions with minimal assumptions about the ideas that people share in common. Individuals may have rich and detailed ideas about the human good, but they cannot expect to make political decisions by bringing everyone to agreement about that. For political purposes, they will require a "thin" theory of the good, encompassing only the most basic needs that everyone shares. Or perhaps, to use another formulation, they will have to accept "value pluralism," recognizing that the goods that reasonable people seek are irreducibly multiple and cannot be ordered in any single system of priorities on which everyone could agree.* But even without a shared account of the good, reasonable people can resolve their disagreements by agreeing to treat each other fairly and leaving a wide space in which to pursue the goods they want, individually or in voluntary associations with others. As it turns out, that minimal, rational idea of justice is quite demanding enough for a society with our unfortunate history of injustices, and the warning of the political philosophers who formulated it is that we will have to settle

---

* John Rawls, *A Theory of Justice* (Cambridge, MA: Harvard University Press, 1971), 395–99; Isaiah Berlin, *Liberty*, ed. Henry Hardy (Oxford: Oxford University Press, 2002), 212–17.

for that, if we want to continue to enjoy democracy in a society as divided in its aspirations as ours is.

The actual course of public discussion going forward, however, bore no more resemblance to this rational pursuit of justice than the fragmented and competing demands for recognition bore to King's ideal of the "beloved community." As pluralism became, at times, quite unreasonable, the attempt to set out terms for public argument may have become too theoretical to give guidance to those who were trying to hold on to leadership in actual political movements. Perhaps, as Michael Sandel suggested, a thin theory of the good that could secure general assent from rational citizens would be too thin to provide arguments that would enable those citizens to choose between the options they actually faced.* In any case, the opposition continued, with no effective framework for reconciliation in sight.

Two decades into the twenty-first century, then, we face again the moment of self-assessment that, as Reinhold Niebuhr warned us, "can only come when the new and just society has been built, and it is discovered that it is not just."** For many, this discovery comes with a sense of loss and betrayal. Some fear that the promise that their children will have better lives than theirs, as they lived better lives than their own parents did, has been canceled. Others measure their shrinking prospects against two or three generations of struggle and conclude that the hope

---

* Michael Sandel, *Liberalism and the Limits of Justice* (Cambridge: Cambridge University Press, 1982).
** Niebuhr, *Moral Man and Immoral Society*, 82.

for equal opportunity will never be realized. These disillusioned groups are divided against one another, and both are set against a meritocratic elite which, though diverse in gender, culture, and ethnicity, is divided into "progressive" and "conservative" wings, each jealous of its own power and determined to prevent the other from linking up with one or more of the disillusioned groups.

Disagreements are less reasonable simply because the exchanges are so brief. Debate, whether in legislatures or in public forums, gives way to bumper sticker slogans and staccato bursts of tweets. The lack of an audience at the 2020 Republican and Democratic conventions, imposed by pandemic conditions, reinforced interest in sound bites that could be repeated in the next day's headlines and news broadcasts, where they would be seen by millions who ignored the speeches in which they were originally embedded. Even in the debates between presidential candidates, with rules that are supposed to elicit focused responses to specific questions, the tactical advantage goes to the zinger that scores a direct hit on the opponent. The intensity of the attack becomes a substitute for attention to the arguments.

There is a growing readiness to insist that dissent threatens to dissolve our democracy in anarchy and civil strife, or, alternatively, that those who want to clamp down on rising demands for social justice aim to replace democracy with authoritarianism. The protests against racism that have filled the streets in Washington, DC, Portland, Chicago, and Minneapolis, coupled with the quasi-military operations mounted against them, suggest that we cannot dismiss the possibility that "America's original sin"* will yet prove to be democracy's undoing. Perhaps, then, we have come to the point where the fragile conditions of "reasonable pluralism" are at risk of disintegration, with no faith or philosophy available to sustain the ongoing arguments that democracy requires.

Polarization

Our divided society seems, however, to fit neither the model of ongoing, reasonable disagreement in our civics textbooks nor the anarchist apocalypse conjured up for us on social media networks. If the end of the twentieth century fragmented our politics, what we are now experiencing assembles the fragments in new ways. In place of fragmentation, we are offered two encompassing orientations, each of which offers an answer to every question, usually by insisting that whatever answer the other side offers must be wrong. We have become polarized.** Our politics is "red" or "blue," conservative or progressive, often without offering any clear account of what makes it one or the other.

If it is difficult to say what defines the poles, it is equally difficult to know what would mark success for their program. The strategic goal is sometimes described as a series of decisive electoral victories after which the other side would cease to be a relevant political force. Former presidential adviser Karl Rove spoke of achieving a

* Jim Wallis, "America's Original Sin: The Legacy of White Racism," *Cross Currents* 57, no. 2 (Summer 2007): 197–202.

** Ezra Klein, *Why We're Polarized* (New York: Simon & Schuster 2020).

"permanent Republican majority,"* and recently some Democrats have argued that their younger, more diverse voter base will secure their future against an increasingly irrelevant Republican minority. But in fact, the opposition is essential. Without the other against which they define themselves, our polarized parties would hardly be able to say who they are. While philosophers and theologians worry about the future of democracy and cast about for symbols and arguments that might resolve the differences, polarization itself has become the stable reality that supports the structure of politics. The threat of disintegration is diminished because each side needs to accuse the other of posing the threat.

The cumulative effect is a substantial change in the way people experience politics in a modern democracy and, indeed, in the way politics fits into the broader culture. While parties and political leaders obviously must adapt to these changes, their effects reach through the whole society and leave all of us trying to understand how the new ways we relate to each other politically also change things in our churches, schools, workplaces, and neighborhoods. When compromise threatens the all-important loyalty of their political base, politicians may decide that Otto von Bismarck's maxim that politics is the art of the possible no longer applies. When Speaker of the House Tip O'Neill said that all politics is local, he was not thinking about maps of a country divided into red states and blue states.

---

* James Carney and John F. Dickerson, "The Busiest Man in the White House," *Time* 157, no. 17 (April 30, 2001): 32.

It may seem at first that polarization encourages political involvement. An oppositional rhetoric encourages you to think you have something at stake, even if you thought politics was mostly about people with money and power pursuing agendas that have little to do with your daily life. The rise of a more oppositional style of politics has been accompanied by a resurgence of populism. Single issues, taken one by one, may not arouse much interest, but when I am told that my whole way of life is at stake, set against a competing, alien alternative, it seems urgent to make my voice heard. Where I do not fully understand some of the issues, social media will provide summaries that can be quickly digested and even more quickly shared.

Polarization thus tends to broaden interest in political issues, but it may result in commitments that are backed up with less detailed knowledge than they might have been when fewer people pursued more focused concerns about immigration, abortion rights, or fossil fuels. Ironically, wider interest in a range of controversial issues may also produce social pressure not to talk about them at family reunions, in the break room at the office, or at the church coffee hour. When a few people were persistent in raising a single issue, the pastor could always delicately suggest an information table in the narthex for those who wanted to know more about migrant labor, or climate change, or drug abuse. When everybody has a strong opinion on everything, the polite alternative may be to say nothing. As more people take positions on a wider range of issues, they may actually have fewer opportunities to hear from others who might disagree with them.

Likewise, at least until the COVID-19 pandemic, the characteristic venue for expressions of polarized politics has been the rally, or perhaps the well-organized public demonstration. These may be boisterous, even rowdy, and somewhat intimidating to outsiders, but most of them will be "peaceful" in the technical sense that they do not require large-scale interventions by law enforcement or result in violence against those who hold other views. The Capitol Hill riot on January 6, 2021, was alarming to many observers on both sides precisely because it served as a warning that these events can easily fall into the hands of extremists.

Most people, however, do not approach demonstrations with an appetite for insurrection. They go to the rally because it gives them a feeling of active identification with a cause, poses few risks, and has minimal opportunity costs. Participants are typically surrounded by those who agree with them, and unlike a public hearing or a lobbying effort, they will not be required to prepare for the event or to explain exactly what it is on which they are all agreed. Being there is primarily a way to acquire an identity, both among those others present and in your own mind. Sporting a hat or a button with a slogan completes the effect and solidifies the sense of accomplishment, especially if it can be documented in a selfie with one of the speakers.

As we noted at the beginning of this chapter, identity is a key to politics, and it is important especially for those who are marginalized, invisible, or discriminated against in everyday social experience. To stand up and be counted as gay, undocumented, or as a person who has been exploited or abused is an important step, and rallies and protests can provide those opportunities. But if identity is hard won, it is also easily exploited. Polarized political events identify you by who you are with and who you are against, rather than by who you are. Being there contributes to the mass enthusiasm that will appear on the news later that night, so that being there becomes its own identity. As the expression goes, "Been there. Done that. Got the T-shirt."

The T-shirt is important for another reason. It suggests the way in which polarized politics has become assimilated to consumer culture, so that choice of party, candidate, or policy can be manifested in clothing, flags, pandemic face masks, and so on. Such expressions are more emotional than political, and less susceptible to argument and critical evaluation. The logo on the T-shirt or the few words on the red, white, and blue sign planted in the yard proclaim a complex of positions and oppositions that we may not fully have taken into our own thinking, let alone prepared ourselves to explain to others. Our reasons for choosing one symbol over another are complex and personal, a mixture of idealism, fear, nostalgia, knowledge, and aspiration that would take us a while to formulate into complete sentences for someone who asked us to talk about them, assuming we could do so without embarrassment. For most people, as we have already noted, consumer politics offers an identity with low risk and low opportunity costs. It is rather like a trip to a big box retail store, where you fill your cart quickly and get out, so that you can return to the places where you can enjoy the life you choose with others who have chosen one just like it.

Weak Arguments and Strong Commitments

All that is innocuous in some ways, and the same point could be made about many important choices that we make for ourselves without thinking them through completely. But a diverse modern democracy depends on making an effort to give reasons for our choices that will be meaningful to anyone who faces the same political questions. That, as we have seen, is part of what the philosophers mean by "reasonable pluralism." Democracy is supposed to be an ongoing argument that moves by reasoned steps from specific policy proposals to larger, shared public goals and then back again from those shared goals to further refinements of policy.

But in a polarized society, nobody is listening. We make our political choices, like our personal ones, in a kind of interior monologue that yields strong commitments and few shared reasons. Some blame this on the rise of social media that give instant access to information that supports our prejudices, but that may be a case of blaming the messenger. New media might just as easily have become a forum for vigorous political disagreement, the way the new print media of newspapers did a couple of centuries ago, when Americans debated the ratification of the Constitution or argued the political questions about slavery in the decades before the Civil War.

I am not suggesting that all of our political arguments need to rise to the level of the *Federalist Papers* or the Lincoln-Douglas Debates. Those were exceptions, even in their times, and they were aimed at larger purposes than their local audiences. No doubt they were tidied up from the rougher arguments that made the rounds in daily conversation and in actual speeches designed to appeal to the crowds of Illinois farmers. But both the published versions and the local stump speeches were *arguments*. They were intended to persuade a public about specific measures that could be explained in detail and connected to basic values that the public would have reasons to share. They were not simply expressions of conviction or declarations of loyalty.

Today, we know a great deal about expressing preferences, but we lack experience in persuading one another with arguments, and we often lack a shared vocabulary in which to make such arguments. As people make their choice between the two great complexes of beliefs and loyalties that divide us, the terms in which a public argument might have been conducted become "branded" like consumer goods, so that they belong to one side or the other. "Justice," "freedom," "choice," and, increasingly, "life" itself become party labels, rather than points of discussion. If we try to argue from a policy proposal to a larger value that supports it, we find when we arrive that the value is already taken, and we cannot use it in an argument without taking on the assumption that we support the whole set of positions with which it is associated. If we argue from a basic value to a policy that puts it into effect, we find that the value is already tied to a host of other policies that express choice, security, opportunity, or whatever value we are working with, and we cannot tether a new one to it without associating it with the rest of them.

Under prevailing conditions, ideas are held up and turned into symbols, rather than argued over as to their meaning and their implications for action. A moment when the president responded to protests by holding up a Bible in front of a church captures the sense that more and more of our shared symbols and values are now understood as available for dramatic gestures that tie them to one side or the other in a polarized opposition. The photo op with the Bible may have been clumsy, but even so it linked evangelical Christianity to Trump's cause and made it at least temporarily unavailable as a starting point for bringing people together.

As the shared moral vocabulary of public life shrinks, public arguments are increasingly limited to matters of economic growth and national security. These, at least, seem to provide public reasons for a course of action, and people on both sides pay attention to the arguments when wealth and safety are at stake. But the pandemic crisis calls even these into question, as economic growth becomes part of a libertarian complex that favors opening things up and gets set against a centralizing progressive agenda that focuses on public health. Neither side finds much reason to pay attention to the other, except to make sure that their opponents do not prevail.

Under these conditions, the idea of democracy conducted under conditions of "reasonable pluralism" quickly fades. Making arguments in terms that everyone can understand and assess, in an effort to define a specific policy that might eventually secure majority agreement, becomes impossible. There are no terms available in which to make the argument, and a "thin" theory of the good becomes too thin to guide real choices.

The task for leadership becomes to offer a broad political identity that still provides a sharp contrast to those who are on the other side. A couple of decades ago, the political parties tried to become a "Big Tent" that could accommodate everybody in a broad, middle-ground consensus. But in a divided society, the tricky assignment is to make the tent large enough for many people to enter, while maintaining the warning that there is still a large and dangerous opposition outside. So one party, call it the "Red Tent," grows large enough to accommodate desires for economic growth and increased security against foreign threats, while the alternative "Blue Tent" swells with those who are concerned with global cooperation and strengthening social programs that provide financial security and access to education and health care. Arguments can still be made in these terms, particularly if they are not too specific about the immediate steps to be taken. But increasingly, what is offered is not a program but an identity.

Each side finds the reasons offered by the other unconvincing or, indeed, incomprehensible, and when we find other people's reasons incomprehensible, it is easy to take the next step and accuse them of concealing the real reasons for their position. They say what they say to conceal the narrow self-interest that lies behind what they offer as public policy. Or perhaps their real reasons are concealed even from themselves, because they have been duped by hostile powers or deluded by their unwillingness to face their own destructive impulses and evil intentions. Sometimes, in fact, the ancient claim that the opponent is a tool of Satan comes in handy, even in the context of twenty-first-century politics.

So our choices become increasingly polarized, and as the prospects for agreement dim, our demands rise in inverse proportion. When politics was the art of the possible, we might settle for a compromise that secured our highest priorities or bought time for further negotiations in the future. When all politics was local, we might accept a loss at the national level if it were compensated by a public works project that brought jobs to town and made things better right here at home. Once politics has become polarized, however, our identity is at stake, and not just our arguments. Nothing less will satisfy us than the entire slate of candidates, the whole agenda of sketchily defined policies, and all of the loosely related goals expressed in the logos on our T-shirts. Our opponents do not just oppose our positions. They threaten who we are. Problems no longer have even proximate solutions. There are only winners and losers.

Part of what is ominous about this polarization is that there are many examples in history where the breakdown of the ordinary frameworks for handling political disagreements have led to grave consequences. We are most familiar, perhaps, with the failure of parliamentary democracy in Weimar Germany that led to the rise of Hitler, the imprisonment and exile of political opponents, and eventually, to the Second World War and the Holocaust. The same dynamics have played out in the rise of authoritarian regimes in many places around the world, with tragic results even when the consequences were not as far-reaching. Some observers take comfort from the fact that in most cases, these things happened in new democracies with shallow roots in the political culture, but the American Civil War was fourscore years in the making, and the stresses of the COVID-19 pandemic suggest that it is not impossible that American democracy could fracture again along lines of race and class that remain unaddressed by our constitutional structures and social practices. The claim that "the future of our democracy is at stake" seems for the moment to be a flourish of polarized rhetoric, but events may yet turn it into a prediction, or a prophecy.

But the lack of solutions for our problems is part of what defines the present moment for our society. Political leaders and ordinary citizens on both sides of our polarized politics address these problems by assigning blame so that it falls on the other side. Thus, paradoxically, both sides need for the problems to continue, since that sustains the sense of crisis on which they both depend.

Politics without Solutions

As we have noted, these tendencies are self-reinforcing. Once begun, the dynamics of polarization elicit responses that sharpen oppositions and demand more and more evidence of loyalty to the new identities they have created. It would be foolish to assign any one cause, such as the emergence of social media, to these pervasive social changes or to blame political leaders, in particular, for encouraging them. What is true, however, is that leaders in every institution and at all levels have had to respond to the changes. Being a politician is different today, but so is being a pastor. Most of this book will discuss how polarization affects churches and other institutions that we do not usually think of as "political." But it is important at the outset to focus on some of the ways that politics has changed.

Organizing and maintaining an electoral majority has always been a fundamental task for politicians in a democracy, but our thinking about that majority has changed in important ways. From the civics textbook idea of positioning your candidate or your program in the center, the dominant strategy today is to rally your base. The more divided the voters are, the more success depends on the reliability and enthusiasm of your core supporters. Conservative Christians pioneered this strategy with the "Moral Majority" movement. The idea was that voters who held conservative religious and social values could be a dominant force if, instead of distancing themselves from politics and social problems, they organized themselves to support candidates who supported their values. Ironically, the key to the strategy was not that these conservative Christians had to have an actual majority of the potential voters. When only some of those who can vote actually do, it is those who are motivated who carry the day. You can win with 34 percent of the vote if a third of the electorate does not vote at all. Their indifference supplies the margin of victory for those who really care about the outcome.

In a polarized electorate, this proves a remarkably successful way to win elections, one that has practically redefined the meaning of "majority" for strategic purposes. Rallying your base ensures that your core supporters will stay with you and generates an enthusiasm that may attract others to slogans and symbols. Once again, the T-shirts are important. Moving toward the center, by contrast, runs the risk of appealing to voters who may still be lukewarm or skeptical, while alienating some of your stronger supporters who are no longer sure you will carry their agenda if elected. It is a familiar part of the underside of American democracy that those who control the electoral process can sway results by setting up districts that isolate minority voters, by making it difficult for their opponents to cast a ballot, or, at the extreme, by outright intimidation. A good deal of the polarized rhetoric of the 2020 election centered on these forms of "voter suppression." But where the margins of victory are thin, as they often are today, maintaining the enthusiasm of your own supporters while the opposition grows bored or distracted may be as effective as the various forms of legal and illegal voter suppression.

Because polarization thus offers a key to winning elections, candidates and their campaign managers can hardly ignore it, whatever their personal feelings about it may be. Once in office, it is still necessary to keep the base together in anticipation of the next election. The general tendency to abuse power by rewarding your friends and punishing your opponents is exacerbated by polarization, since your opponents are unlikely to be won over no matter what you do, and your friends may well see conciliation as a sign of weakness. Polarization reduces responsiveness to new issues, and it discourages compromise. Particularly when different branches of government are under control of different parties, the result may be paralyzing political dysfunction. Government shutdowns when necessary spending authorizations are not passed become a regular occurrence, along with prolonged delays when negotiations over essential legislation reach an impasse. In short, under conditions of polarization, the constitutional processes by which our democracy chooses leaders and divides power between different branches of government may no longer be adequate to provide the goods which government must supply or to sustain the good of society itself. We become better at seeking office than at governing.

As American society has become more sharply divided in recent years, the evidence has grown that polarization threatens the system of government and the electoral processes on which that society depends politically. Faltering legislative responses, failure to prepare for and respond to inevitable and predictable natural disasters and pandemic diseases, and ongoing legislative disputes about how to finance health care and other essential human services all warn that normal disagreement may be giving way to polarized oppositions that cannot carry on a public argument about how to resolve the problems.

Nevertheless, it is important to remember that politicians did not create polarization alone. It grew as they adapted their practices and institutions to its exigencies, like everyone else. One might argue, in fact, that this adaptation has been highly successful, pitting one extreme against another to produce an ongoing, relatively stable version of polarized politics, instead of the catastrophic breakdown that previous history might lead us to expect. Government shutdowns close the national parks and the Library of Congress, but no one turns off the lights in the Pentagon. Dealing with the COVID-19 pandemic devolves to the states, where governors and mayors somehow devise responses framed as polarized oppositions between themselves and federal authorities, or between themselves and public health experts. The same dynamics work at the local level for clashes between police and protesters. Polarization is the new normal.

Perhaps there is no other way to govern at the moment, since the forces that led to polarization clearly continue. The question is not whether political leadership has adapted to polarization, since everyone has had to do that. A more nuanced question is whether, in adapting, they have taken on practices that undermine the political system on which we all depend. Have they successfully adapted to polarization for larger purposes? Or has polarization taken them over the way a virus exploits its host, so that the host becomes an instrument of its own destruction? As it turns out, that may be a timely way of putting the question for all of us.

The Church in a Polarized Society

The polarization of American politics in the first two decades of the twenty-first century marks an important movement beyond the uneasy cultural and political unity of the 1950s, the protest movements of the 1960s and 1970s, and the fragmentation into single-issue politics that marked the end of the century. The prevailing strategy today seems to aim at consolidating a base toward one end of the political spectrum and identifying everyone else as the opposition.

These political divisions increasingly reinforce divisions in the broader culture, as people take on identities shaped by the polar oppositions. Yet in the details of their lives, most people get on with regular routines of work, family, and worship, marked by predictable patterns of consumption, including their consumption of political identities. This is not quite what John Rawls meant by "reasonable pluralism," but it does work reasonably well, at least until some outside event like a terrorist attack, a global economic crisis, or a pandemic disease reveals just how ill-prepared our governments are to do what governments are supposed to do.*

But the question we need to ask, as suggested at the end of the previous chapter, is not whether polarization works in the sense that it allows life to continue. The question is how our adaptations to it are changing us and changing our institutions. We have reviewed some problematic effects of polarization, as parties become more focused on winning elections than on governing and as the loss of a shared moral vocabulary reduces the chance for real arguments about policy. But what about the churches and other communities of faith in this divided society? How are they adapting, and what is happening to them in the process?

Adaptations

The decades of change that led to our polarized politics also had their effect on congregations and denominations. Beginning perhaps as early as the 1950s, ecumenical and interreligious dialogue strengthened ties between religious groups, and the white Protestant proprietorship of American religious life gave way gradually to a more open and diverse image of what it means to be people of faith. Most importantly, this opened the way for religious leadership to take a prominent role in the Civil Rights Movement and for historic Black churches to move be-

---

* Francis Fukuyama, "The Pandemic and Political Order: It Takes a State," *Foreign Affairs* 99, no. 4 (July-August 2020): 26-32.

yond their well-established role at the heart of local communities to become centers for economic development, urban renewal, and educational reforms that reach across entire cities. As the movements that culminated in voting rights and other civil rights legislation continued on into a long, hard struggle for economic and social change, religious groups took on new roles that continue central to their mission today.

These were important developments, not least because they drew a younger generation eager for changes into a new kind of religious leadership. The centers for social services and community development and the networks of congregations that support them continue to anchor many urban neighborhoods, and they have become more essential where public services have deteriorated. But in retrospect, we have to say that these developments were not as transformative as they seemed to many at the time. Larger changes were under way, and the comfortable place that the churches occupied at the center of American life shrank along with the center itself.

Many of these changes were unintended consequences of larger demographic shifts. As churches expanded along with the suburbs in the 1950s and 1960s, they were often planned to replicate the neighborhood and parish churches familiar in the older cities. Every few miles would see a new Methodist or Presbyterian congregation, a Lutheran congregation transplanted from its original city location, a Catholic parish and school no longer identifiable with a specific immigrant community, and African Methodist Episcopal or Baptist congregations springing up in new suburban outposts of African American professionals, educators, and skilled workers. But with time, as people grew more mobile and sought their entertainment at multiplex theaters and did their shopping in sprawling retail malls, they went farther afield for religious community, too. A favored style of worship and a comfortable fit with the other worshipers became more important than mere proximity, often more important than denominational labels. Like other activities, church became a destination that offered an identity, and this identity was more individual and self-chosen than when your church was your parish or a place like the place where your grandparents worshiped. This new religious individualism sustained some congregations, while others fell by the wayside. Many of the suburban churches of the 1950s have developed distinctive styles of worship, youth programs, or social ministries that draw members from a much wider area than their builders could have originally imagined. The more successful have expanded their facilities with preschools and activity centers and auditoriums, and some have moved on further to construct new megachurches.

Others, of course, struggle to survive, and some close every year as their aging congregations can no longer maintain their programs, leadership, or facilities. Mainline Protestantism, especially, experiences this decline, and clergy and congregations are continuously on the lookout for new programs, new slogans, and new symbols that will attract attention and perhaps revive the interest of the growing numbers who are deciding that they are "spiritual but not religious." But one of the hazards of dealing with decline is that we can become so focused on our own problems that we fail to notice how they are connected to other things going on around us. One of these connections is a significant parallel between the religious identities that draw people to successful congregations and the development of consumer politics that supports the polarized political identities described in the previous chapter.

In today's divided society, churches must deal with demographic changes, changing attitudes toward organized religion, and the increasing pressures felt by many families just to earn a living, keep their finances together, and keep their children safe. For local congregations, the easy assumption that the church has a secure place in community and family no longer works, and they struggle continuously to adapt worship, program, and outreach in response to changing needs and expectations.

In many places, clergy and lay leadership take on this task with creativity and dedication, and with real success. The church now seems likely to outlast the shopping mall, the local newspaper, organized labor, and maybe even the suburbs, not because it remains unchanged, but because it adapts. But it is important to step back from the immediate demands of adaptation and ask the question we keep returning to: Has the church successfully adapted to a changing society, or has a divided society exploited the church for its own purposes, remaking it to fit neatly into the polarized identities now available?

A Church That "Takes Up Space"

The church has faced questions like this many times in the past, and a wider perspective may give us a clearer view of our present problems. One point of reference that often resonates with thoughtful contemporary Christians is the situation of the church in Germany in the 1930s, in the years just before the Second World War. There, too, economic problems and social unrest demanded change, but a courageous group of theologians, church leaders, and Christian activists worked together to keep the church from adapting to the militarism and nationalism that were sweeping through German society at the time.

The figure of Dietrich Bonhoeffer (1906-45) has particular appeal to American Christians. His leadership in the German church, the part he eventually played in a conspiracy against Hitler at the highest levels of the German government, his execution in a concentration camp, and the writings on theology and ethics he left behind have made a compelling story ever since it became known shortly after the end of the Second World War.[*] It helps with the American audience, too, that this highly educated, well-placed son of a prominent German psychiatrist also studied at Union Theological Seminary in New York, found his way to the Abyssinian Baptist Church in Harlem, and drove across much of the United States in a borrowed Oldsmobile before catching a train for a brief excursion into Mexico. Bonhoeffer seems well positioned to help us understand how the church can be of

---

[*] The first authoritative biography of Bonhoeffer was written by his student and collaborator in the Confessing Church, Eberhard Bethge, *Dietrich Bonhoeffer* (New York: Harper & Row, 1970). An excellent recent account is Ferdinand Schlingensiepen, *Dietrich Bonhoeffer, 1906-1945: Martyr, Thinker, Man of Resistance* (London: T&T Clark, 2010).

use in many different contexts, and we will want to follow his thinking for some distance in our reflections on the church's adaptations to a divided society. But we will also need to stop before we come to the end to remember that our divided society is significantly different from his and to ask ourselves what difference that makes for our churches.

Adolf Hitler's regime that took power in 1933 moved quickly to see that its political ideas and its centralized leadership structure were duplicated in all institutions of society. For Bonhoeffer and other Protestants who opposed this extension of Nazi domination into the churches, an essential step was to create alternative structures for church leadership and for the education of pastors. They formed a "Confessing Church" that announced its intention to remain faithful to the historic statements of the Christian faith, in contrast to the "German Christian" movement that enthusiastically embraced a nationalist and anti-Jewish version of Christianity. Bonhoeffer became the director of one of the seminaries of the Confessing Church, gathering a small group of students on an estate at Finkenwalde, in an isolated area where they could, at least initially, avoid notice by the authorities. The design the new director had in mind for this seminary went well beyond the preparation for preaching, church leadership, and pastoral care that we might usually associate with a seminary curriculum. To avoid giving in to the new ideology that was reshaping their society, these young pastors would need first to shape a way of life for themselves before they could make use of practical skills in ministry.

Bonhoeffer's plan owed much to the Catholic concept of "formation," an extended period of time during which catechumens, novice members of religious orders, and candidates for the priesthood learn the life they are entering by living it with others who share prayers, study, and life in community. For most of the young Protestant students who joined Bonhoeffer's seminary, this was a new thing, very different from what they were expecting. They responded to the experience with enthusiasm, and many of them adapted the idea for the congregations they eventually served. In 1938, Bonhoeffer wrote *Life Together*, a short book based on the experience at Finkenwalde, and it, too, gained wide attention in the difficult days just before the Second World War. Several years later, Bonhoeffer was surprised to find that it had been used as a common reading by the monks he visited at a Benedictine monastery in Bavaria.*

What Bonhoeffer rediscovered for his students and then for his readers was the presence of God in ordinary life. Life at Finkenwalde was designed to show how the relationships and activities in everyday life can be seen as part of God's creation. This was an important idea at a time when many German lives were still disrupted by the effects of the First World War, economic collapse, and the political chaos that brought Hitler to power. But it was also a controversial idea, especially in Protestant theology at the time, because many of the leaders of the

---

* Dietrich Bonhoeffer, *Conspiracy and Imprisonment, 1940–1945*, Dietrich Bonhoeffer Works, vol. 16 (Minneapolis: Fortress, 2006), 113.

Confessing Church had a very different understanding of the relationship between faith and daily life. Instead of a formation that made use of everyday experience to shape the Christian life, they put the emphasis on God's transcendence of all human ways of ordering life. To hear the Word of God, we must be prepared to hear God's judgment on all the ways we live, including the ways we live our faith. This was an answer to those who saw Germany's defeat in the First World War and the subsequent collapse of many of its social institutions as a threat to Christian civilization. We need not listen to leaders who summon us to restore Germany's place in the world, because God's judgment stands above all such human loyalties and values.

Bonhoeffer was initially drawn to this theology of judgment, which he also saw as an answer to the cultural self-confidence he detected in American theology and to the racial prejudice that was built into much of American Christianity. When he returned to Germany after studying in New York, he looked not to the older theologians who had been his teachers in Berlin, but to Karl Barth, whose "crisis theology" took the unsettled times as a sign of judgment that required new attention to the Word of God. It was no accident that Barth became one of the leaders of the Confessing Church, or that Bonhoeffer was among the younger pastors whom these leaders looked to for the future.

But there was another theme in Bonhoeffer's work that was in some tension with Barth's emphasis on God's transcendence of all our human categories of judgment. In his brief career as a professor of theology in Berlin, Bonhoeffer had lectured on the biblical themes of creation and fall, and he explored the idea that God's command is present in the world God created for human life, just as God's judgment is evident in the world when this created order is ignored.* This was an idea to be approached warily, because it could easily be put to use by the Nazis to support their claims that the natural order included Aryan racial superiority and an all-powerful state like the one Hitler was creating. Barth preferred to exclude such ideas from his theology altogether.**

This tension between God's transcendence and God's creation would occupy Bonhoeffer's thoughts in all of his later theological writing, and it comes down to us as part of the legacy of his unfinished work.*** But in practice, he seems to have realized immediately that if there were a risk that the German Christians would misuse the idea of a life ordered by God's creation, there was also a risk in abandoning that idea to them, for in their interpretation of the order of creation, the call to join the movement that Hitler led could be presented, not just as a political decision, but as an ultimate choice, by which all of life could be ordered. Then it would make sense to demand that the principles of National Socialism apply, not just to law and government, but in universities, churches, and every social institution, right down to the level of family life. That

---

* Dietrich Bonhoeffer, *Creation and Fall: A Theological Exposition of Genesis 1–3*, Dietrich Bonhoeffer Works, vol. 3 (Minneapolis: Fortress, 1997).

** Karl Barth, *Nein!* (Munich: C. Kaiser Verlag, 1934).

*** Dietrich Bonhoeffer, *Ethics*, Dietrich Bonhoeffer Works, vol. 6 (Minneapolis: Fortress, 2005), 388–408.

kind of ultimate choice could be presented to fearful and confused people whose lives had been disrupted as the one way to restore meaning and purpose to their lives.

What Bonhoeffer's students learned in their experience of Christian formation was that God is known not only beyond human life, but also within it, in the details of everyday living, in ordinary relationships, and especially in a shared community of prayer. As Bonhoeffer would put it later, the church of Jesus Christ "takes up space" in the world.* By this he meant, of course, not just the physical space of church buildings or the old house in Finkenwalde that the seminary occupied, but a space in the world that is different because of people whose lives have been formed by their faith. The church cannot be reduced to interior contemplation that makes no difference in action, nor can it be absorbed into a political program that claims to order everything in its own terms. The life of faith brings order to a chaotic world and disrupts the order that worldly powers try to impose on it.

The Church against the World

But how, exactly, do we take up space? In Hitler's Germany, the mere existence of the Confessing Church defied the order that the government was attempting to impose on the churches. Eventually the police decided that the seminary in Finkenwalde took up too much space, and

---

* Dietrich Bonhoeffer, *Discipleship*, Dietrich Bonhoeffer Works, vol. 4 (Minneapolis: Fortress, 2001), 225.

they shut it down in 1937. But even within the space the
Confessing Church created, there were questions. How
should they respond to the increasing persecution of the
Jews? If war came, should seminarians and pastors join
in the defense of their country or resist military conscrip-
tion? Some of Bonhoeffer's students ended up in prison.
Others were killed in military service. For Bonhoeffer
himself, as is well known, those questions eventually led
him into active collaboration with a small group of highly
placed Germans who sought to kill Hitler as a necessary
step toward the overthrow of the Nazi regime.

Resistance, however, could take many forms, even
within the Third Reich, and Bonhoeffer seems to have
understood that the kind of conspiracy in which he became involved was not a possibility for most Germans
who were opposed to the regime. At one early point in
his work, he considered the possibility of visiting Gandhi
in India, to seek guidance about a movement of nonviolent resistance like the one King would later undertake in
the United States. But under the circumstances in Germany, he concluded that the most important resistance
available to the Confessing Church was simply its continued existence. To "take up space" was in itself an act of
defiance against a regime that insisted on controlling all
space for itself, from the top down.

That kind of resistance captures the attention of many
readers of Bonhoeffer today, as they find themselves in a
world that increasingly feels alien, if not actually hostile
to Christian faith. Where earlier generations might have
hoped for a social transformation based on biblical ideas
of peace and justice, or at least seen themselves as com-

fortably part of a "Judeo-Christian" culture, many now doubt that their values are shared, or even understood. A divided society seems to offer no place to the faith that once tried to hold it together. Theologians, pastors, and church leaders turn instead to ideas of a church in resistance, which takes up space not by changing the world, but by stubbornly refusing to go away.

A full account of the ways this idea of resistance has been taken up by the churches in our divided society would fill a book in itself. We can, however, briefly sketch two different approaches to this growing sense of fundamental opposition between Christianity and the wider culture. One is more activist, making use of law and mobilizing public opinion to protect a Christian identity that it sees as under threat. The other is a strategy of withdrawal, emphasizing the irreducible differences between a political society organized by coercion and a community of love that may exist within political society, but can never be part of it.

Resistance through Religious Freedom

A more activist form of Christian resistance to our polarized society is often found among evangelicals who participated in the political movements of the 1980s. The religious activism of that era, as we have seen, aimed at broad social changes, and newly energized evangelical groups like the Moral Majority had hopes of making political gains that would enact culturally conservative policies and give a prominent place to their version of the

Christian heritage that shaped the nation's institutions. Their leaders could envision successes that would match the transformative effects of the Civil Rights Movement a decade or so earlier.

As transformative hopes among conservative Christians gave way to the polarization we know today, the idea of a powerful evangelical voice that had too long been politically inactive was traded for an image of Christianity under threat from dominant forces of secularization. The task became less to project Christian values into the wider society than to protect what is left of the heritage of a Christian nation from those seeking to dismantle it. An agenda originally shaped by contemporary culture wars has come to include a distinctively Christian account of American history, with a particular place for Christian practices and values built into the nation's institutions from the beginning. From that vantage point, the separation of church and state and the religious tolerance that treats all religions equally and gives equal respect to those who hold none of them are not our founding principles, but radical interpretations imposed on law and government in an attempt to exclude Christianity from the public square.

At this point, the movement's values and symbols become part of a strategy of resistance that takes up space by remaining visible despite the fact that dominant cultural and political forces are arrayed against them. The idea that secularists are waging a "war on Christmas" may seem overstated, but it allows those who hold it to turn even the traditional "Merry Christmas" greeting into an act of defiance. Culturally conservative understandings of marriage and family, teaching from the Bible and prayer in public schools, and display of religious symbols in public spaces receive intentional support, not because these Christians expect them to be generally observed and adopted, but as a sign that they have a place and will not be forgotten or abandoned under pressure.

The idea of religious freedom plays a prominent part in this resistance.* The refusal to bake cakes or provide flowers for a gay wedding is a way to mark resistance, as is the refusal to provide employees with insurance coverage for medical services such as abortion or contraception that violate the employer's beliefs. Efforts to secure legal protection for these positions on the ground that they are expressions of religious freedom serve the dual purpose of asserting the principle and locating it deep within the nation's history. If the "free exercise of religion" permits choices that would not be allowed for any other reason, then the law itself acknowledges that we are from the beginning a religious, even specifically Christian, nation.

This broad interpretation of religious freedom runs counter to a legal history that has extended generally applicable laws to cover religious observances, too. In that interpretation, religion is protected only from state actions that are specifically targeted against it. Laws that forbid discrimination or mandate health coverage apply generally, even to those citizens who have religious objections to them. In recent years, the conflict between these

---

* Thomas C. Berg, "'Christian Bigots' and 'Muslim Terrorists': Religious Liberty in a Polarized Age," in *Law, Religion, and Freedom*, ed. W. Cole Durham et al. (London: Routledge, 2021), 164–88.

two understandings of the scope of religious freedom has inspired a sort of legal tug-of-war between a limited interpretation embodied in many court decisions and broader views embodied in legislation intended to undo the court decisions.* But for religious groups who build their resistance around an idea of religious freedom, the ongoing legal controversy only serves to reinforce the point that a full expression of Christian identity faces secular forces that seek to limit it.

A legally nuanced account of religious freedom might be part of a strategy of litigation or legislation, just as the Civil Rights Movement took an understanding of equal protection of the law into the courts and legislatures. But the main point of many current assertions of religious freedom seems to be the resistance itself. A carefully selected provocation, such as refusing to bake a cake, will serve that purpose better than a campaign of legislation or litigation. The main purpose is not to persuade the skeptical, but to guide action for those who share these beliefs, so that they can integrate them into the details of their lives and make them part of the way they see the world. The assertion of religious freedom is less political and legal than it is a program of Christian formation. The point is not that the ideas become more widely accepted, but that the resistance they shape continues to take up space.

* For an overview of this contrast, compare the Supreme Court 1990 ruling in *Employment Division v. Smith* (494 US 872) with the Religious Freedom Restoration Act (107 Stat. 1488) enacted by Congress in 1993.

Resistance through Witness and Withdrawal

A second contemporary form of resistance has roots that go back even farther in history and offers a more fully developed theological account of its distinctiveness. Its idea of nonviolent Christian community can be traced back to the Radical Reformation and the sectarian groups that formed self-contained communities separated from both state and church in the places where they first formed. If they sometimes found a home in the tolerant New World of religious freedom emerging in North America, they nonetheless kept their distance from the institutions of law and government in their new homeland. It was perhaps inevitable that in the fragmentation of the late twentieth century, this older resistance, with its strategy of withdrawal, would have new appeal to some theologians in mainline traditions as they became disillusioned with the results of twentieth-century religious activism.

After a burst of Social Gospel enthusiasm for personal transformation as a source of social change and a brief consideration of pacifism after the First World War, American churches and clergy had generally adopted the rule of law as the means for social change and the use of force as a moral instrument in international affairs. But the persistent social unrest and resurgent political conservatism that led up to our contemporary polarization led this group of Christians to rethink their understanding of church and society and, indeed, the whole idea of theology.

For this strategy of resistance, the church exists as a witness to God's judgment on a social order organized

by self-interest and violence. While Christians sometimes speak of the church as the "conscience" of society,
this is a mistake if it implies that they could correct and
improve the world around them step-by-step, one problem at a time. What is important is not the good work
the church might inspire others to do or undertake on its
own, but the judgment proclaimed by its existence as a
community of love that makes no sense when measured
by the standards of the world. We are called to witness to
the Word, not to witness to what the church can accomplish. The church that counts its successes in numbers,
dollars, new buildings, and new programs does not "take
up space" in a world that measures effectiveness in those
same terms.

This idea of the church's witness as a strategy of resistance makes an important statement at a time when
many congregations struggle with declining numbers
and aging membership, and it offers encouragement to
clergy whose idea of pastoral leadership extends beyond
trendy worship and contemporary music. But if it is clear
what we are not trying to measure, it is less clear how we
will recognize this witness where it exists. Few congregations have consciously sought to make this idea central
to their identity, and although we have noted its historic
connections to the Radical Reformation, some have recently connected it to a "Benedict Option," recalling the
monastic movement that withdrew from a disordered
world at the beginning of the Middle Ages.* The church

---

* Rod Dreher, *The Benedict Option: A Strategy for Christians in a
Post-Christian Nation* (New York: Sentinel, 2017).

as a community of witness does not seem to imply any one way of worship or denominational tradition. Perhaps it exists as a shadow presence that takes up space *within* the churches as much as it takes up space in the world.

Whatever symbols and liturgies are employed, proclamation will be central to community that exists as a witness to the Word. But in this, too, the resistant witness will be careful not to confuse faithfulness with effectiveness. There must be no invitation to an easy discipleship that demands little more than warm feelings while we hold hands around the communion table. Nor will there be sermons that deal in what the theologians call "apologetics," an explanation of the faith in terms that answer questions you were already asking. Indeed, theologians sometimes speak of this proclamation of the Word as having its own "grammar," which must be mastered to use its terms in the right way. Understanding is not just a matter of acquiring a few new words. It is like learning a whole new language. To ask whether the proclamation will be persuasive to someone who thinks in the ordinary categories of economics, sociology, science, or philosophy is to miss the point. For those whose understanding is not already shaped by the Christian proclamation, what Christians have to say may not even be comprehensible.*

As with the resistance built around religious freedom, the point of contact between this resistant strategy of witness and Bonhoeffer's community of seminarians

---

* George Lindbeck, *The Nature of Doctrine: Religion and Theology in a Postliberal Age* (Louisville: Westminster John Knox, 2009); Stanley Hauerwas, *With the Grain of the Universe: The Church's Witness and Natural Theology* (Grand Rapids: Brazos, 2001), 15.

at Finkenwalde is an emphasis on formation. Becoming a part of the community means maintaining everyday life in a distinctive way. Whether against the ideology of Hitler's Third Reich or against the relentless pressures of a secular consumer culture, Christians must discipline themselves to hear the Word before they try to proclaim it. That is what the church is for, and we find it where this formation happens. The church does not exist in symbols, buildings, denominational affiliations, or social programs. The church takes up space where people come together to stand apart from the world around them and measure themselves against different expectations.

Resistance and Polarization

Different as they are from one another, both of these movements tell us some important things about contemporary theology and about the divided society in which we find ourselves. Though they focus their attention on different problems, they share the judgment that the world around them is moving in the wrong direction. A society that once provided an environment for a life lived according to Christian values now poses a threat to that life. Christians must secure a space for their faith by turning the structures of religious freedom, which are still in place in the law, against a society that no longer believes in Christian life nor, really, in religious freedom. This seems a desperate last-ditch effort of resistance, though no more desperate than the strategy of resistant witness that concludes that the societal commitment to

justice that the church helped to shape is a bad idea.*
If resistance once meant marching for justice, Christians
must now resist by withdrawing their support from the
coercive and violent means that governments deploy in
the pretense that they are enforcing justice.

Certainly, these two versions of resistance do not
offer a common vision of what society ought to look
like. What they share is resistance to the directions politics and culture have taken since the 1960s, and this
includes resistance to developments in the churches.
While the Moral Majority led conservative evangelicals
into political activism in the 1980s, the contemporary
movement seems to focus chiefly on acts of resistance
to a general expectation that secular ideas about marriage, sexuality, education, and family life will prevail,
with little hope that a mobilized Christian constituency
could change public policy on these subjects by political means. The witness to a Word cherished and understood within a Christian community likewise finds
the strategies of earlier Christian activists irrelevant to
this new community. Changes sought through politics
may, indeed, achieve justice understood in political or
economic terms, but such achievements will be limited
and fragile, and as Karl Barth put it many years before,
"In no sense can they ever be even a first step toward
the Kingdom of Heaven."**

---

* Stanley Hauerwas, *After Christendom? How the Church Is to Behave If Freedom, Justice, and a Christian Nation Are Bad Ideas* (Nash-
ville: Abingdon, 1991).

** Karl Barth, *The Epistle to the Romans*, trans. Edwyn Hoskins
(London: Oxford University Press, 1933), 517.

The Confessing Church, absolutely clear about its differences with the political ideology that was enforcing its control on the society around it, provides an attractive model for these contemporary Christians disillusioned with all of the ideas about social witness, conservative or liberal, that might have seemed plausible a decade or two ago. The idea that the church does the most important thing it needs to do simply by continuing to exist is an appealing thought when you are surrounded by the wrecks of more ambitious plans. In addition, it offers the attractive image of Dietrich Bonhoeffer as an individual, who, quite apart from his understanding of the church, has been pressed into service as preacher and prophet, pacifist and potential assassin, conservative champion of individual freedom and progressive voice for religious tolerance and racial equality.*

There is appeal in heroic figures like Bonhoeffer and others who resisted Hitler. They are examples of integrity who may be admired in any circumstances. There is also a certain resonance between the way they refused to be taken in by Nazi propaganda and the ways that our contemporaries reject worldviews that contradict their faith,

---

* As the number of witnesses who can remember what Bonhoeffer himself said and did is diminished by age and death, the variety of Bonhoeffers who offer themselves to literary imagination seems to grow. The counterforce to this is a new generation of scholars who read Bonhoeffer in his own theological context and give us a theologian who is important precisely because he is *not* talking about our problems. See Michael DeJonge, *Bonhoeffer on Resistance: The Word against the Wheel* (Oxford: Oxford University Press, 2018); Joshua Mauldin, *Barth, Bonhoeffer, and Modern Politics* (Oxford: Oxford University Press, 2021).

even when those worldviews are widely represented on the Internet and on the street. But apart from a general admiration for people who are willing to stand up for what they believe in, it is hard to see how resistance to an authoritarian state tells us much about how to deal with our divided society.

Whatever terms we might use to describe Nazi Germany—fascist, authoritarian, totalitarian, tyrannical—we cannot say that it was polarized. The regime that took power in 1933 moved quickly to bring all institutions under its control and to suppress anyone who questioned its ideology. To "take up space" was to run a real risk, as it is in any authoritarian society.

In our case, opposition is not only tolerated. It is almost universal. Whatever sets itself up as an authoritative claim about what we Americans should believe, what we ought to do, how we should view our past or plan our future will call forth a contrary position that puts as much distance as possible between itself and its opponents, challenges their facts, and impugns their motives for making the claim in the first place. Polarization more or less requires this reflexive resistance.

An authoritarian system strictly limits dissent and suppresses any mass opposition. In a polarized society, the entire system depends on raucous opposition that clears out the middle ground and drives everyone toward the poles. One favorite way to do this is to claim that your opponents are so fixed on their erroneous ideas that they want to set up an authoritarian regime to enforce them, but few really believe they are seriously planning this, or that it would even be possible. Intellectuals of a leftist bent, noting that our polarized government cannot even get itself together to control a pandemic disease, will occasionally speculate about whether authoritarian states do this better than we do. Those on the right are likely to blame an authoritarian state for letting the disease loose in the first place. Thus, the debate about polarization itself becomes polarized.

A church that wants to take up space by setting out to resist such a culture is welcome to do so. It can hardly be prevented from trying. But the result is apt to be something like what happens to the two versions of resistance we have just examined. The activist evangelical resistance asserts religious freedom against new laws that threaten historic Christian beliefs and practices. Resistant witnesses reject the use of force and withdraw from the Christian nation that activist evangelicals seek to restore for their own purposes. These forms of religious resistance in a polarized society are themselves caught up in the polarization.

Adaptable or Exploited?

What happens to resistance in a divided society is a reminder that polarization is a pervasive social reality to which everyone adapts. Religious leaders seek to witness to the presence of the ultimate in the midst of life, but that witness inevitably gets bent in the direction of poles in a wider social opposition. Congregations and denominations sort themselves out along these lines, or they divide into rival camps within themselves, but like all institutions in the polarized society, they continue to function at some level. Those who, like the resistant witness, attempt to withdraw from the system altogether still end up being assigned a place within it.

The relevant question, as we noted at the beginning of this chapter, is not whether we will adapt to polarization, but whether we will be exploited by it. For the church, it is important to see that a strategy of resistance lends itself to exploitation. History provides us with many examples of Christians who stood against persecution when kings and emperors claimed all power for themselves, and the resistance of the Confessing Church is a recent case where, just by continuing to exist in the midst of German life, the church provided a witness that the Nazi state was not the ultimate reality. But in a polarized society, to stand against one way of looking at the world will simply be taken as an endorsement of another. To reject state coercion and violence lumps you together with every other critic of existing power, and in a polarized society, there will be many of them. To assert freedom to live according to evangelical Christian norms makes you part of a challenge to all the changes that have reshaped social, familial, and race relations over the past few decades, including changes for which many Christians have worked and prayed.

The various movements may intend their resistance to convey a more nuanced message, but the nature of a polarized society works powerfully against that. The church "takes up space" in a world that says, "Take all the space you want. Nobody is listening. We will locate you at the appropriate pole in our polarized worldview and move on." Resistance thus fails as a strategy for the church's primary task of witness to the ultimate reality in the midst of ordinary life. In a polarized society, all commitments take on a tinge of ultimacy, because they become part of the identities that define progressive against conservative, faithful against faithless, patriot against globalist, "us" against "them." Or perhaps, in a polarized society, no commitments can bear witness to ultimate reality, because in that society, political identities come cheap. Each side is eager to take anyone who is still wandering in the middle into their own idea of who "we" are, and the T-shirt is available to anyone who wants one. Attempting to "take up space" in that contentious environment results in being taken into someone else's space.

Bonhoeffer's abrupt withdrawal into the seminary community at Finkenwalde, after his wide-ranging explorations of American church and society, his involvement in European ecumenism, and his academic recognition by leading scholars and theologians, serves as a reminder that political, social, or economic powers that claim ultimate authority for themselves may appear in history with little warning, and the need to reorder our lives to resist them is a part of the church's mission that we must not forget. But we must be cautious about moving too quickly from our divided society to Bonhoeffer's resistance. If the only way we know to be the church is an idealized version of the Confessing Church in the 1930s in Germany, we will need to find ourselves a Hitler to resist, and by identifying someone as the Hitler we need, we will end up contributing to the culture of polarization that we intended to resist.

The Penultimate

We need a different way to take up space. Fortunately, Bonhoeffer himself suggests how we might do this in the way that he organized the community at Finkenwalde to focus their formation on the details of ordinary life. His seminarians prepared themselves to proclaim the Word of God, not just by practicing their sermons, but by living together. They shared their prayers and their problems, ordered the hours for work and study, provided for meals, and learned to serve one another in ways that respected both those who gave and those who received. The way they did this was unusual, living in community and apart from the rest of society, but the things they were concerned with are part of ordinary life for everyone—for people in the churches where they would preach, and for us today.

Bonhoeffer would later call these "the things before the last" (*die vorletzten Dinge*). His translators have usually turned to a more obscure English word, *penultimate*. The word has Latin roots that refer to the thing that is just before the last thing in a series. The word is ordinarily an adjective, referring to particular things that come before the last things; but in theological terms, it can become a noun, *the* penultimate, referring to the whole complex of things that are part of ordinary experience, things which clearly are not ultimate, and yet which have a definite relationship to God as Ultimate Reality. To speak truly and clearly about the ultimate, we must also understand what is penultimate, both in how we act toward it and how we speak of it. Bonhoeffer included a whole chapter on this in the ethics text he began to write in 1939, after war broke out and he had been forbidden to preach or teach publicly.*

As we noted earlier in this chapter, other theologians were more cautious about this interest in the penultimate. In a time of demonstrative patriotism, extreme nationalism, and glorification of the nation's *Führer*, it could seem best to emphasize God's transcendence and call into question any effort to find a point of contact between human purposes and ultimate reality. Bonhoeffer shared that concern, but he saw that in a larger view of the Christian witness, relating the concerns of human life to the reality of God is a risk that must be run. God is the source, guide, and goal of all that is (Romans 11:36).** Christ "takes up space" not only in the incarnation, and in the church, but also in the realities that make human life possible and give shape to our relationships in the world. God gives significance to these penultimate realities as we build our lives around work, home, worship, friends, and family. As people of faith, we experience their connection to the ultimate, and when these penultimate goods are missing, everyone feels their absence.*** Bonhoeffer understood that while we must be careful not to confuse ultimate and penultimate things in our politics, we cannot eliminate the connection between them in our theology.

But our time, too, has a problem with ultimate and penultimate things, though it takes a different form from

---

* Bonhoeffer, *Ethics*, 146–70.

** The "source, guide, and goal" theme runs through the whole of Miroslav Volf and Matthew Croasmun, *For the Life of the World* (Grand Rapids: Brazos, 2019).

*** Bonhoeffer, *Ethics*, 98–102.

the one Bonhoeffer and his contemporaries faced. As with other aspects of our polarized politics, penultimate things are drawn to one or the other of the poles, and the space in between is emptied of concrete goods. Health, housing, employment, safety, and even faith and family all belong to one party, and they are all put at risk by the other side—take your pick as to who you want to tell the tale.

We need not suppose either of these contemporary parties has the totalitarian ambitions that Bonhoeffer faced. Indeed, it seems unlikely that they do, since the political system and those who hold power in it have come to depend on this polarized confrontation. But what happens when penultimate politics is elevated to ultimate reality is much the same as what happened in the middle of the twentieth century. Health, housing, employment, safety, faith, and family lose their concrete reality and have significance only in relation to a political identity that secures them against the forces that are said to be poised to destroy them. We lose the capacity even to talk about penultimate things in shared, public terms, because they have all become connected to a political ideal that sets itself in opposition to any but its own way of thinking about them. Ironically, this has the result that the more we depend on a polarized political identity to give us our orientation to these penultimate goods, the less our political leaders need to tell us about how they will deliver them to us. Policy proposals no longer receive critical scrutiny, and policy positions become increasingly vague. The important thing is not how the leaders of our party will deal with the penultimate things that make up the details of our lives. The important thing is that they will protect those things from the other guys.

What Bonhoeffer understood was that the theological task is not only to maintain the distinction between the ultimate and the penultimate, but also to take the penultimate seriously on its own terms. That is what prevents the penultimate things that make up daily life from being taken up into an idolatrous ultimate, whether there is only one available idol, as in Hitler's Germany, or two, as in our polarized politics, or more. Indeed, one possible future for our divided society is that it will fragment into a multipolar world with even more possibilities for understanding *us* against all the rest of *them*—with even more hats and T-shirts to go around. But the basic theological and pastoral problem of maintaining the importance of the penultimate against a self-proclaimed political ultimate will remain much the same.

The penultimate is where human life is lived. It is diminished when it is not related to the ultimate, but it is distorted when it is prematurely absorbed into an ultimate, even when that ultimate is the genuine ultimate reality of God, but especially when it is a political pretender to ultimacy. Christian theology explains this in terms of the importance of the incarnation. We take the penultimate seriously because Jesus entered into it and used its familiar elements as parables of the kingdom of God. But the need for the penultimate is obvious in more ordinary terms, as Bonhoeffer understood:

> The hungry person needs bread, the homeless person needs shelter, the one deprived of rights needs justice,

> the lonely person needs community, the undisciplined
> one needs order, and the slave needs freedom.... To give
> the hungry bread is not yet to proclaim to them the grace
> of God and justification, and to have received bread
> does not yet mean to stand in faith. But for the one who
> does something penultimate for the sake of the ultimate,
> this penultimate thing is related to the ultimate.*

What becomes clear here is that in relation to what is truly
ultimate, the penultimate always retains its integrity. Only
leaders who seek to raise their own importance in history
to the level of a false ultimate need to diminish the penultimate by absorbing it into their own purposes. We do not
feed the hungry to make America great again or as a first
step in a program of economic equality, but because the
hungry person needs bread. Bread, justice, shelter, and
community are goods which we create in the activities
of ordinary life. The church takes up space as Christians
work with others to fill the world with these goods. It also
takes up space by insisting that penultimate things are related to God and to each other, so that they do not need a
political program to give them their significance.

Concrete Goods

The penultimate is made up of specific, concrete goods
that shape the lives of particular individuals and communities. Each person sees bread, shelter, justice, and com-

* Bonhoeffer, *Ethics*, 163.

munity in a unique way, and the meaning of these things varies accordingly between communities, cultures, and different times in history. Sociological generalizations and moral ideals are useful for organizing our thinking, but they cannot tell us very much about the penultimate if they are simply imposed on it. Understanding penultimate things is a matter of building relationships, not only between the penultimate and ultimate reality, but between penultimate things themselves.

By building these relationships we come to understand how penultimate things are made and what their good is. This is different from understanding what they are good *for*, in terms of the use we might make of them or how we might market them in a consumer society. The "thing" here might be a specific material object, simple as a clay pot or complex as a computer. But it might be as large and multifaceted as an urban neighborhood, a government office, or a school, composed of many different things and people in multiple relationships. The point is to understand what is necessary for *this* thing to come together and continue in existence as a good, functioning clay pot, a good pharmaceutical company, or good Centers for Disease Control. We want to understand the relationships between the various goods that are necessary to bring a penultimate good into being and the various goods that are possible when it successfully does what it is meant to do. To fully understand those relationships, we must also know what penultimate goods cost, not in abstract terms of dollars and cents, but in the other goods we must be prepared to give up, delay, or diminish to have this concrete good, now. These questions about concrete goods came into stark relief at the beginning of the COVID-19 pandemic, when we had to decide how to weigh the good of an economy that was functioning and growing against the good of limiting the spread of a virus and having health care services available for the larger numbers who were suddenly in need of them. The fact that these choices immediately became the subject of political controversy was a warning just how polarized our society has become.

By contrast, understanding penultimate things as concrete goods related to one another and to ultimate reality takes them on their own terms. Of course, we deal with them from our own point of view. The complexities are such that we could hardly understand them at all if we did not start from where we are. But thinking about concrete goods requires making specific judgments about what is good for ourselves and others and articulating those judgments in terms we might share with others, rather than reducing goods to subjective wants in the way a consumer culture does. This way of speaking about concrete goods, then, is necessary to the theological task of relating the penultimate to the ultimate, and it provides a starting point for a different way of thinking about politics. Our polarized, dysfunctional politics prefers the space between its poles to be empty of concrete goods, allowing at best a few "thin" goods on which everyone can agree, but which do not do very much to help us make real choices. All the real human goods that matter can then be accumulated around a political ultimate. By contrast, the church seeks to proclaim the ultimate in relation to penultimate things. To do that, we must learn to speak meaningfully about concrete goods on their own terms, within the penultimate.

Ethics

A comprehensive account of penultimate things in relation to the ultimate and of the multiplicity of concrete goods in their connections to one another is obviously a complex subject. Theologians have developed many systems of ethics to provide what is wanted, speaking about the connection between ultimate and penultimate as the orders of creation, or as laws of nature, or with even less reverence for them, as structures of life by which God preserves a sinful humanity from its own disordered impulses. Practical philosophers might object that such an account of concrete goods is impossibly detailed, and while it might serve the purposes of a highly impractical theology, the attempt to understand everything in relation to everything else is of no use *within* the world of penultimate things. (Some of these philosophers might add a claim that this is the only world we know, or that it is the only world there is.) Theological critics might also detect a note of pride in the undertaking, since an account of the penultimate in the terms just outlined would require a comprehensive knowledge of the order of creation *and* its relationship to the Creator. But a realistic theologian might reply that faith in God as ultimate reality does not demand that the faithful produce a complete account of creation. Faith is trust that God is the ultimate reality in whom all things are related, so that the concrete goods in the world of our experience are related to God and can be known in part by those who are attentive to them. It is precisely because we cannot give a complete account of all human goods that we must take an interest in each of them.

To this defense of an ethics of concrete goods, we might add that most people intuitively approach the world in this way. They are moral realists. They do not think of a good life as an idea that they can impose on the world as they find it. They expect to learn what is good in experience, creating concrete goods out of possibilities given in their own situation and maintaining these goods by their choices among equally real alternatives. A meaningful life consists of concrete goods, secured over time by habits that help us make the right choices about them and by relationships in which the goods can be sought and shared together. Ethicists might devise ways to talk about how that life is meaningful by calling the habits "virtues," and theologians might call the human relationship in which goods are sought and shared together "love." But people have loves and virtues whether or not they have a vocabulary for them, and they find what they know of lasting happiness in the concrete goods and the connections between them that have proved real in their own experience. This kind of moral realism has been around for a long time. The paragraph you have just read would serve as an introduction to Aristotle's *Nicomachean Ethics*.

From Aristotle's time to now, however, most people who read and write books about ethics have not fully recognized just how pervasive this thinking about penultimate goods is, and how deeply it is built into the

structures of everyday life.* That is where the ethics of
Jesus makes a difference, by taking seriously ordinary
experiences, making parables of things that everybody
encounters, and building relationships that reach all the
way from lost coins and lumps of yeast to the ultimate
purposes of God. Aristotle thought that you need a pretty
wide range of choices and a lot of free time to think about
them in order to understand the good. But we should
know from experience, if not from what the Gospels try
to tell us, that it is often those whose options are few who
see most clearly what really matters.

To be sure, there are those whom the need for food,
shelter, or justice is so overwhelming that questions about
other goods and the virtues that sustain them have no
practical meaning. For these most urgent needs, as Bonhoeffer says, "it would be blasphemy against God and our
neighbor to leave the hungry unfed while claiming that
God is closest to those in deepest need."** But for most
of us, who hold on to concrete goods with varying degrees
of security and sufficiency, the moral and theological task
is to develop a deeper awareness of both how we create
and maintain penultimate goods and how all those goods
and all the people who create them are related to God.

This cannot be done by proclamation alone, any more
than we can say to a person who lacks food and clothing, "'Go in peace, be warmed and filled,' without giving
them the things needed for the body" (James 2:16). It re-

---

* For more on the possibilities and limitations in Aristotle's ethics, see the section "A Circle of Responsibility" in chapter 4 below.
** Bonhoeffer, *Ethics*, 163.

quires a detailed knowledge of how concrete goods are created, where the resources required for them may be found, and what sorts of collaboration effectively bring them together. That is to say, we cannot proclaim the relationship between ultimate and penultimate things without enlisting all sorts of people who can help to take up the space required to hold penultimate goods together in meaningful lives. The skeptical, secular philosopher who insists on keeping attention focused on the penultimate has something to contribute. So, too, does the political philosopher who seeks a thin theory of the good that will provide a common denominator for everyone's search for the good. The effort includes value pluralists whose list of concrete goods may be short but is also irreducibly multiple. It includes millennials whose relation to the ultimate is "spiritual but not religious," persons of other faiths, and persons of no faith whose practical wisdom and depth of commitment to their neighbors speaks to us of God, even if it does not speak that way to them. We even need those who cannot organize the miscellaneous collection of goods and relationships in their personal experience into a meaningful life unless they get their T-shirts and join themselves to a political identity that tells them that what they value is under threat.

The church discovered in the course of the Civil Rights Movement, if we had not known it before, that we share a common cause with everyone who seeks justice. Today, we must go beyond that to acknowledge that this common cause includes everyone who seeks to name, create, and maintain concrete goods. The diversity among those involved in this serious moral thinking is wide, and many of the disagreements between them are important. But to seek agreement on everything would only contribute to the division and polarization that is putting concrete goods at risk for many people. Even those with whom we disagree may know important things about specific goods and relationships, and we must take them seriously for what they know, even if they do not know that they know it.

Formation

As the church seeks to understand the relationships between penultimate and ultimate things, we need to be alert for unexpected wisdom in unfamiliar places. Nevertheless, the obvious place to start is with the experience of those who are already in our churches, or who might be there, if they had not been turned off by assertions of a hostile religious freedom or confused by the declaration that they will probably find what we have to say incomprehensible. There are many concrete goods created at choir practice, in church kitchens, and around the circle in discussion groups, scheduled or spontaneous. The COVID-19 pandemic helped us see how much we need these goods by depriving us of them for a while, but it also demonstrated their importance through the resilience and creativity devoted to keeping them going online and in alternate ways.

But even among those whom pollsters would identify as "regular churchgoers," we should not assume that they grasp the connections between the goods they intuitively seek and their church experience. Religious affiliation, as we noted, is often a kind of consumer identity. It takes its place among the ways people tell themselves and others who they are, and they value the experiences of worship and fellowship that they get from it, but they may not suppose that the rest of their experience has much to contribute to it. The churches have adapted so well to the polarized society that churchgoers will not ordinarily be challenged by the views they hear or the people they meet there, and in the absence of a shared framework for public argument or theological discussion, their faith may be more a matter of subjective satisfaction than a way to put the pieces of their life together for themselves or make that comprehensive vision effective in their relationships.

The problem, then, is not just that many Christians have become reticent to talk about their faith in our divided society. Nor is the problem solved when some become all too eager to talk about it, making Christian faith one more marker of the ways we are polarized. The connection between ultimate reality and penultimate goods does not become real by hearing someone talk about it. The church must provide a context where it becomes real in experience. That is to say that the first task, especially in a society that tends to redirect the life of the church to other purposes, is *formation* around the church's own purpose, which sees connections where others are constructing oppositions and thus builds unity in a divided society. People who have taken up Christian faith as a consumer identity and learned the ways they live it as part of a polarized politics must be given an opportunity to connect the penultimate to the ultimate in ways that begin in their own experience, in the details of their own lives.

Formation begins with giving people a different way to relate to the concrete goods with which they are most immediately engaged. We can make some guesses about what those goods are once we know where they work, how they live, and what their family life is like. But unlike Bonhoeffer, who could structure the whole experience of daily life for his seminarians, formation in the church today is mostly a matter of asking questions and really listening to the answers. The concrete goods that are most important are the ones that people in their own experience create and maintain. When they know that, they have begun to understand how these goods are related to other goods and other people, not in some instrumental way that serves their own needs or as part of an ideological construction that pits one set of goods against another. Formation means finding ways to share the experience of concrete goods. Formation is listening when no one else is doing it.

Precisely because this runs counter to the way that a divided society locates concrete goods in its polarized framework of meaning and purpose, formation requires some shared disciplines and a community in which it can happen. There is necessarily some conscious distance between the church and the rest of society. The resistant witness that separates the community of faith from the surrounding culture is right about that, at least initially. But the community of formation does not exist only to maintain that distinction between itself and an uncomprehending world. Nor is its work limited to resistance against the forces in society that would use it for other purposes. The task of the church in our situation is something different. The church locates itself in the moral void that a divided society tries to create between its polar alternatives. The church announces to the world that that space is not empty. What the divided society will find there, taking up space, is not only the church, which was supposed to have relocated itself to one or the other of the poles, but the beginnings of that public moral discourse that seemed to have disappeared altogether.

PART II

Listening

The polarization of contemporary politics inspires editors, commentators, and politicians themselves to warn about an impending crisis for American democracy. Yet with each election cycle, our divisions become more predictable, stable, and comfortably familiar. That is not to say that polarization makes our politics better. Loss of trust, refusal to compromise, and dependence on an electoral "base" that is quick to reject any attempt at conciliation make it difficult for government to get anything done. But we adapt. Political leaders manage to get themselves reelected. They pass essential legislation with only an occasional, "partial" government shutdown, and when a real crisis arises, they manage to respond despite the rituals of mutual recrimination. The rest of us adapt, too, in our places of work, our local communities, and in our churches.

But the adaptations come at a cost, as our individual identities and group commitments are absorbed into red states and blue states, conservatives and progressives, globalists and patriots. Each pole views the other side with undifferentiated hostility and increasingly casts a suspicious eye on the less militant members of its own group. The more polarized we become, the more it seems that individuals and groups must somehow learn to mirror these divisions in order to retain their place in the divided society.

Congregations and clergy, too, have to live with the world as they find it, but adaptation to a divided society clearly cannot be their only goal. As we saw in the previous chapter, a polarized worldview that sees everything at stake in the differences that separate *us* from *them* gives rise to easy identities and false ultimacy. Christian faith, by contrast, proclaims a God whose ultimate unity transcends all human differences and whose presence in Christ enters into the details of human life with created purpose and redemptive possibilities. In a divided society, the church has to offer something more than a Christian version of polarized identities. To put the matter in Dietrich Bonhoeffer's terms, the church must "take up space" in a different way.

We might begin by listening, since no one else is doing it. This may seem like dangerous advice when the church faces strong adversaries. When people are uncertain of their convictions, there is a risk that if they listen, they will be persuaded by those who are more sure of themselves. But in our divided society, there is remarkably little persuasion going on right now. Both sides have their minds made up about a wide range of issues. Those who are on our side do not need to be persuaded. No point in bothering them with arguments; they are already wearing the T-shirt with our logo on it. The point is to give them something to cheer about. Nor is there any point in trying to persuade the other side. We have a theory that explains why they are victims of their own false consciousness, why they could not understand, even if they tried. Surely, there has rarely in our history been a time with so much certainty and so little real discussion.

Listening, then, might suggest that something else is possible, that an argument might be heard, if someone cared to offer one. But openness to argument is only one part of the attitude that I characterize as listening. Before listening is about persuasion or being persuaded, it is a matter of understanding. It involves a readiness to go beyond first impressions and surface differences to discern connections between people and experiences across time and distance. Listening is acquiring a way to think about things that seem too large to grasp, or too small to be worth a name. Listening is the way we approach the world when we are not trying to do something we already want to do or tell somebody what we already think.

Especially in a divided society, the church's work of formation is about listening to the Word of God in a way that makes it possible for us to listen to one another. By listening to the Word, we learn to see God as the source, guide, and goal of all things (Romans 11:36). Listening to one another means listening to those with whom we create and maintain the concrete goods that make ordinary life possible. Then, we need ask who is missing from these conversations and what they might have to say if we were listening.

In these chapters, then, we will ask how the church in a divided society might listen to the Word of God (chapter 3). That will provide a starting point for asking also how we might listen to the world (chapter 4) and listen to those who are not heard (chapter 5). In each of those inquiries, I will suggest some ways that the church can stop simply adapting to polarization and recover its own purposes. By suggesting how the church can "take up space" in these ways, we may also begin to see how our presence might help the whole society move beyond our present divisions.

Listening to the Word

Listening to the Word of God is the central activity of the church in worship, prayer, and study. Indeed, it might seem that listening is inevitable, when week by week lessons are read from the Bible, expounded in sermons, recast in hymns and anthems, and echoed in prayer. But all that involves a good deal of talking and not necessarily very much listening. Really listening to the Word of God is different. It jolts us out of our own doing and telling and relocates our egocentrism in a *theocentric* reality.*

It is tempting to say that when we listen to the Word of God, we understand everything differently, but it may be more to the point to say that we no longer think we understand *everything*, precisely because the reality of God escapes the familiar assumptions that we use to organize our lives and even the words we use to pin down the finite things that make up our ordinary experience.

---

* See, for example, James Gustafson, *Ethics from a Theocentric Perspective*, vol. 1, *Theology and Ethics* (Chicago: University of Chicago Press, 1981).

To use the terminology of theologians, God transcends the world, and the Word of God escapes the categories we use to make our way through the world and explain it to ourselves. So, God is both a loving parent and a righteous judge, both present in all things and beyond them, both the origin from whom all things come and the ultimate reality to whom nothing can be compared. To use another theological term, even our most precisely formulated ideas about God are *apophatic*, both true and not true at the same time. If faith is at risk from materialistic accounts of the world that seem to render God unnecessary, it is also at risk from affirmations that rely too much on particular verbal formulations, whether drawn from scripture, creeds, or the sermons of persuasive preachers. To get at apophatic truth, we must understand that words which reveal God to us also reveal what we do not know about God, ourselves, and the world.*

Listening to the Word of God is thus much more than sitting through a sermon or lifting ourselves out of a bad mood with a few words from scripture and a verse from a favorite hymn. The words, as Karl Barth put it, must become the Word. "The Word of God becomes knowable by making itself knowable."** Hearing the Word is an event in which the Word creates its own hearing, and in that event both the words and the hearer are transformed in ways that cannot easily be captured by adding more words to the occasion.

---

* For a valuable summary of the history of this tradition of "negative theology," see Douglas F. Ottati, *A Theology for the Twenty-First Century* (Grand Rapids: Eerdmans, 2020), 291–96.

** Karl Barth, *Church Dogmatics* I/1 (Edinburgh: T&T Clark, 1936), 282.

Much of our hearing is a matter of learning new things about realities that exist apart from ourselves. Whether we just learned something about Mars by reading a book on space exploration or just heard something from a neighbor about a new grocery store, the point is to figure out this thing in relation to other things, to locate it, pin it down, and give it a place in our world. Hearing the Word of God is different. In this hearing, we know God in and beyond all things, not as another thing we can locate among the rest. Nor does this hearing give God a place in our world. It would be more to the point to say that we begin to find our place in God. We become who we are by responding to this Word, which calls us into being as surely as it called all things into being at creation (Genesis 1).

The theologian H. Richard Niebuhr (1894–1962) summed this up by describing the human person as "the responsible self," constituted by a kind of knowing that shapes us in response to who and what we know.* We usually speak of "responsibility" in relation to other persons to whom we have special obligations. Or we may talk about our responsibility as citizens, or the responsibilities that go with membership in a congregation, or holding a job, or other relationships. These varied settings where we have responsibilities are important, and we

---

* H. Richard Niebuhr, *The Responsible Self* (New York: Harper & Row, 1963). H. Richard Niebuhr's theological account of responsibility influenced twentieth-century American theology in much the same way that his brother Reinhold's Christian realism shaped American social ethics. See above, pp. 10–12. See also William K. Schweiker, *Responsibility and Christian Ethics* (Cambridge: Cambridge University Press, 1995).

will have a good deal more to say about them in the next chapter, when we talk about "listening to the world." But Niebuhr's "responsible self" involves much more than accepting the responsibilities that go with our situations, doing what we have been asked to do or what we have committed ourselves to doing. Being a "responsible self" includes those tasks and duties of everyday life, but hearing the Word of God involves encountering God's action in every experience and being ready to respond to God's action as we encounter it in that event. The responsible self affirms, "God is acting in all actions upon you." Beyond fulfilling our roles and obeying the rules, we become who we are by responding to all actions upon us so as to respond to God's action.*

If that seems to make listening to the Word a moment of insight or a special religious experience, we must not forget that what happens in the hearing is an ongoing transformation of the hearer, in which the scattered and often broken experiences of everyday life are understood in new ways because they are all related to the ultimate reality of God. A theocentric worldview is not only about realities that transcend our experience. It is also about finding connection to God in small things and ordinary relationships, so that things that seemed too small to notice or that were to us merely instruments of our own purposes also speak of their Creator. In relation to what is truly ultimate, as Bonhoeffer understood, the penultimate has its own significance. We do not need a political ideology to give meaning to family, work, and culture, and

---

* H. Richard Niebuhr, *The Responsible Self*, 126.

we can let politics do its distinctive work without needing an enemy to give our politics a purpose.

So, the implications for our divided society already begin to be apparent. But let us not move too quickly to politics. The first task for those who listen to the Word of God is theology, even for those who are not sure they know what theology is and who are still trying to figure out what *apophatic* means.

Faith, Hope, and Love

The purpose of theology is to understand the world and our own experience in theocentric terms. The history of doctrine and systematic theology can be important aids to this larger task, especially the ideas about a triune God who is our Creator, who redeems us in Jesus Christ, and who is present to us in the Holy Spirit. But even for those who spend their lives as pastors and teachers working with these terms, refining ideas is not the goal. What Christianity provides instead is what James Gustafson (1925–2021) calls an "orientation" or a "posture" toward the world. Charles Curran calls it a "stance," which perhaps makes the point best, because it suggests a person who takes a position in preparation for action.[*] To know God as the source of being, order, and meaning in all things is a way of life, rather than a set of ideas. We live

---

[*] James Gustafson, *Christ and the Moral Life* (Louisville: Westminster John Knox, 2008), 242; Charles Curran, *The Catholic Moral Tradition Today: A Synthesis* (Washington, DC: Georgetown University Press, 1999), 30.

in relationship to our experiences and to other persons as they are related to God, and we act accordingly.

Our theology becomes effective in dispositions and habits that shape our actions. We approach the conflicts, contradictions, and defeats in life with faith that what seems absurd or evil nonetheless has a place in the reality that God has made and will ultimately redeem. This faith sustains hope that what now is incomprehensible and broken may yet be made clear and whole. Hope, in turn, frees us both to love those who sustain us and to love our enemies, even when loving them requires hope that they may change. These dispositions to faith, hope, and love are traditionally known as the "theological virtues." They are drawn together already in the New Testament (1 Corinthians 13:13). Catholic theology, especially, emphasizes that these virtues are gifts from God, for without God, who is the ultimate source of being and meaning, we would not be able to sustain the faith, hope, and love by which this ultimate reality becomes real in our own limited experience, where so many things seem to contradict it and where so many other "ultimates" compete to be the center of our being and meaning.

In the next chapter, we will consider how relating all things to God involves relating things and persons to one another and how the theological virtues of faith, hope, and love relate to other, more ordinary virtues such as patience, honesty, and courage that we might acquire in the course of our experience. First, however, we need to connect this somewhat idealized picture of a responsible self whose faith is poised for action to the present reality of the church in our divided society.

Formation

The familiar language of faith, hope, and love might lead us to think that the theological virtues come naturally to Christians, at least to those who are regular participants in the life and worship of the church. But we should not assume too much. As we have noted, when people are not listening, they come to expect brief and simple answers. Our society often treats identities like consumer goods—easily available, requiring little maintenance, and quickly exchanged when they begin to show signs of wear. That is unrealistic for any identity that really makes a difference in the lives of those who carry it, and it certainly does not fit the gospel accounts of what it means to follow Jesus by taking up the cross and being willing to lose our life in order to find it (Luke 9:23–25).

But churches, too, adapt to consumer identities. In our culture, people who show up at public events and popular venues expect to hear things that will make them feel good about themselves for being there, and they tend to carry that expectation with them when they show up at church, too. Pastors ignore that at their own risk. Books and sermons about faith, hope, and love slip easily into the idioms of self-help manuals. The advice may still be good in everyday, practical terms, especially for people with self-defeating habits who most urgently need the help. But self-improvement is not quite the same thing as understanding all things in relationship to God as the source of being, order, and meaning. The opportunities to present a theocentric understanding of reality in an hour or two on

Sunday morning are limited, and the pressures to restate it in more familiar, self-centered terms are considerable.

It is at this point that the case for withdrawal into a distinct community of Christian formation becomes most compelling.* We cannot assume that even those who are regular participants in the life of a congregation will have a framework in which to construe their Christian commitments apart from a divided society in which they are told over and over that they must be vigilant about protecting their own interests and alert to the threats posed by those with different identities and loyalties. It may seem impossible to listen for the Word of God without withdrawing from this overwhelming social confusion into an alternative community, even acquiring an alternative "grammar," in which a very different truth can be spoken. With so many other words available that compete for attention with the Word of God, even active, committed church members need a community of *formation* to bring faith, hope, and love to effective expression in their lives.

Unlike Bonhoeffer's seminary at Finkenwalde, however, our churches must undertake this formative task in the midst of competing messages and multiple obligations, rather than in a community of formation that keeps its distance from them. This is a practical necessity for most pastors and church leaders, who can only ask for so much attention from busy mothers, part-time college students, stressed-out gig workers, and managers with deadlines to meet. Bonhoeffer's lessons from the Finkenwalde community set out in *Life Together* may be

---

* See above, pp. 51–54.

a good text for the Thursday study group, but it does not describe a life that its members can expect to lead, set apart from all the other places where they try to make sense of their faith.

In addition to the practical limitations of a strategy of withdrawal, there is a way in which it contributes to the temptations of a divided society, rather than providing an alternative to them. Withdrawal into an alternative community lends itself to polarized oppositions that set one group against another—we who are serious against those who are not, we who are practical about our Christianity against those who think they are better than we are. In a divided society, a distinctive community of formation that sets itself apart may thus end up contributing to the problem it was supposed to solve. Instead, listening for the Word today begins with the delicate tasks of listening to people who may not be listening to one another and raising questions without arousing hostility. Small groups with fluid boundaries and short duration may serve this purpose better than well-defined intentional communities, especially if they are followed up with pastoral concern for those who may be left with new questions or who are trying to figure out their next steps. The COVID-19 pandemic, which forced congregations to connect people through new media and in different combinations, may provide innovative models that will be useful beyond those immediate needs.

At the same time, we should remember Barth's axiom that "the Word creates its own hearing." A sermon series or a Bible study on "listening for the Word of God" misses the point if it tries to do the listening for the congregation.

Bible study needs to provide enough background so that participants do not read Leviticus, Hosea, or Mark as if the text had been written last week, but too much help with the application to their own lives misses the point of studying it as the Word of God. Good sermons and good music serve the work of formation, too, especially if they are offered in an environment that does not present the church as a refuge from contemporary life. At this point in our history, many people will arrive with a readiness for a different way of seeing things. God may show them what they are seeking, if we do not try too hard to tell them what that is.

Another way that the church in a divided society may try too hard to do the listening for its people is to become a recruiting center and staging area for various forms of social activism. In contrast to a strategy of withdrawal that gathers a community of formation within the church, this approach turns people around almost as soon as they enter the door and points them outward to find God in movements for justice that challenge established powers and call attention to needs that go unmet. Like the prophets in the Hebrew scriptures or like Jesus challenging the legalism of the scribes and Pharisees, the church that hears the Word of God in this way responds with urgency, even impatience, to pious words that mask indifference to human suffering, especially when that suffering serves the interests of those who ignore it.

In most American churches, this activism has an important place that dates back to abolitionism, women's movements, the development of Catholic social teaching, and Protestant advocates of a "Social Gospel." More recently, Black churches were central to the social transformations of the Civil Rights Movement, and social justice ministries that date back decades are sponsored by local, regional, and national denominational bodies. Activist churches do more than point people out the door and into the streets. Church leaders accompany them, and often when they arrive at the demonstration, clergy will be at the head of the march. The way that our ideas of Christian formation have expanded to encompass these social issues is one of the most important achievements in church life over the past century.

Nevertheless, the developments that led to today's divided society have changed the way that the questions of social justice present themselves, and it is not clear that the churches' commitments have kept pace with the changes. Half a century ago, Martin Luther King could lead a campaign for civil rights that would, as it gained momentum, embrace other disenfranchised groups, all those whose opportunities were limited by poverty, and a broad coalition of people seeking to end the war in Vietnam. Today, identities are more fragmented and more competitive. Before joining the march, everyone wants to know who is going to be represented among the leaders. A general commitment to "peace and justice" highlighting a different issue each month with bulletin inserts supplied by the denomination's Church and Society agency may pass largely unnoticed, even by those it intends to lift up. In any case, the emphasis now is on identity, rather than solidarity, and nobody wants to have justice done for them. To have recognition, I must claim it for myself.

Theocentric faith thus has the hard task of equipping the church with the habits of faith, hope, and love without telling its members who they are, what to think, what to do, or worse, telling them what the church is going to do for them. In a world now crowded with identities, Christian faith must be more than another way to claim one for yourself. It must be a different kind of identity, where those who provide leadership leave space for people to hear the Word for themselves.

Faith

Belief in a God who is maker of all things is a disposition to seek unity, even where unity is not evident and especially where it is denied. Science and religion, diverse traditions and cultures, different faiths, and even different politics all are part of one reality, which has its origin in God. There is much to be learned from studies in biology, anthropology, philosophy, and comparative religions that see similarities that are not obvious on the surface, but theocentric faith traces all things back to God, so that even when we cannot see the connections between them, we trust their place in a good creation. Sometimes that trust is hard to come by, even for ourselves. That is part of why a Christian identity, or indeed any human identity, is more difficult to achieve than a consumer culture makes it seem. But theocentric faith trusts God's love, rather than our own goodness, so that despite what we know about ourselves and what we may find out if we dare to ask, we can be who we are.

The corollary to this theocentric understanding of ourselves and the world is an affirmation of God's love for others, however we encounter them. It is sometimes hard to love the people we live with every day, let alone those whom we know only as images on a television screen or see as nameless individuals grouped together by a label. But we need to remember that it is not how we experience them that connects them to a loving God. The connection to God is there, quite apart from how we see them. Theologians used to speak of "forensic justification" to insist that God's grace might, like a judge in a courtroom, simply pronounce someone righteous, without producing any visible evidence of personal transformation and newness of life. There are theological problems with a doctrine of grace so thoroughly disconnected from the experience of grace, but perhaps "forensic justification" is a model for thinking about how we relate the world to God, even if it is not a complete account of how God relates to the world. We pronounce that the connection is there, even when we cannot see it and when the other people with whom we have to deal at the moment provide us no evidence for it. Forming people in a theocentric faith involves providing opportunities for these experiences that run counter to their prejudices and intuitions. To understand the world in relation to God, it is sometimes necessary to suspend our own judgments about the world and how we think God sees it.

Hope

Because theocentric faith sets before us a world that we do not fully understand, it is important to connect that faith with hope. For the church in a divided society, that is a particularly difficult task. The polarized, oppositional worldviews that dominate contemporary politics often lack any expectations for the future that do not begin with the defeat of the opposition. Some may call this anticipation of victory "hope," but it does not extend very far into the future, and despite efforts to energize their base for a sweep of the ballot, political leaders depend on continued opposition to explain their own resistance to compromise or to any reconsideration of their positions. Over time, these attitudes can give rise to a defensive posture that is susceptible to conspiracy theories and unable to acknowledge defeat. Genuine hope yields to a kind of political paranoia that expects the worst, and the most committed partisans begin to doubt the possibility of a democracy that includes those who disagree with them. For those not engaged by this polarized rhetoric, confusion and disappointment can give way to disillusionment and withdrawal into a private world of work and family where political choices no longer seem to make any real difference. This, too, suits a polarized political leadership, as long as the disillusioned and withdrawn would likely have voted for their opponents if they had remained involved.

Today, almost every congregation includes people who have experienced these dislocations, and there is an urgent pastoral need to address their rage, fear, and disillusionment. It has been recognized that political extremism poses threats to mental health. Today's polarization extends those risks more widely through the society, disrupting personal relationships and affecting the well-being of those who no longer relate to what seems to be happening in the world around them.* But the theological virtue of hope is not about mental health. Hope is trust in God's presence and power in history, as well as confidence in the world's reconciliation in God at history's end. God's reign is this future that faith anticipates, even when we know that human actions—including our own—frustrate God's purposes.

Like the listening to the Word that leads to faith, formation in hope cannot be reduced to proclamation alone. An exhortation to be hopeful, like an exhortation to be cheerful, is apt to produce the opposite effect. It calls attention to what is absent, and the one to whom the exhortation is directed may conclude that the one who exhorts does not really understand the problem. Hope grows as people have opportunity to reflect on their own experiences in light of the biblical witness to death and resurrection and parables of the Word as the seed that grows while we are sleeping (Mark 4:26–29). Small-group discussion and prayer are essential accompaniments to worship and preaching for receiving the gift of hope, as they are for the theological virtue of faith.

Hope, however, is also an important goal of educational programs, especially in a divided society where

* Richard Hofstadter, *The Paranoid Style in American Politics*, introduction by Sean Wilentz (New York: Vintage Books, 2008). Hofstatder's classic analysis of political extremism was first delivered in 1963 and traces developments in American politics in the 1950s.

continuous news feeds maintain our attention by rein-
forcing fear. Hope takes a longer view of history in which
defeat is sometimes a necessary accompaniment of judgment, but exile is followed by return. Those themes in
the Hebrew Bible can be reinforced by studies that follow
the history of the church through periods of decline and
renewal—Saint Francis's move from the monasteries to
preaching in the streets, John Wesley's revivals during a
disruptive period of social change, and the transformation of inherited prejudices by recent movements toward
freedom and equality.

These long cycles of history often have parallels in
stories of decline and renewal in local communities and
in individual congregations. Retrieving and document-
ing these experiences can be an important ministry, both
for the congregations directly involved and for those
who pass the story on through wider networks in church
and society.*

Hope requires acquaintance with figures like Dietrich Bonhoeffer and Martin Luther King Jr., whose tragic
deaths proved in the end to advance God's reign and left
an enduring witness to purposes that their opponents
sought to wipe out of history. Hope also grows from the
stories of ironic reversals in which what appears weak
proves strong and forces that seemed firmly established
in power end up dependent on those they sought to control. Hope that relies on God does not require public con-

---

* See, for example, Joseph T. Reiff, *Born of Conviction: White
Methodists and Mississippi's Closed Society* (Oxford: Oxford University Press, 2016).

firmation. It is content to escape through a hole in the wall and be let down in a basket (2 Corinthians 11:32–33).

Hope is the narrow gate in our polarized society (Matthew 7:13–14). There are broad highways of anger and disillusionment that veer to the right or to the left and lead to places where low expectations about the world and other people are confirmed. The church must resist opportunities to fill the pews by appealing to these prejudices, but it must also lift up examples in its history and in contemporary experience that form people in theocentric hope. Theocentric hope trusts that what God is doing is greater than our polarized judgments can capture. When we respond to God's action on us, we may hope to accomplish more than we intended and to see responses from others that we did not expect. The first step in sharing that hope more widely may be our own hope that it is possible.

Love

Love is the greatest of the three enduring theological virtues (1 Corinthians 13:13), and formation in love is central to the life of the church. That involves understanding God's love as the constant and unchanging foundation for our changing affections, loyalties, and enthusiasms, so that we are led away from seeing the world and other people as alien or as potential threats and begin to love them as God loves them.

God's constant love, however, takes form in us through our human nature, which limits us in changing ways at different times. A church which ignores those limits may wind up telling people to love everyone, everywhere in a way that offers warm feelings and good intentions where a real response to God's love might require planning, action, or even a little prophetic anger. As Christians developed realistic approaches to the problems of the twentieth century, they recognized the difference between "moral man" and "immoral society," between our capacity to love one another in intimate groups and personal relationships and the structured obligations that must govern the larger society, independently of how we feel about those who share it with us.* As Reinhold Niebuhr put it, justice is "only an approximation of brotherhood. It is the best possible harmony within the conditions created by human egoism."**

We have already noted, however, that seeing social relations in formal terms of law and impersonal standards of justice can obscure the important differences between persons, and of course, when we reduce love to the requirements of justice, we hand a good deal of power to the scholars, lawyers, and legislators who tell us how justice works. Love increasingly struggles to recognize the differences in society and to hear what other people have to say. Love under conditions of finitude seeks justice not just *for* others, but *with* them.

---

* Reinhold Niebuhr, *Moral Man and Immoral Society* (New York: Charles Scribner's Sons, 1932), 3–22, 257–77. See also Harvey Cox, *The Secular City: Secularization and Urbanization in Theological Perspective* (New York: Macmillan, 1965).

** Reinhold Niebuhr, *The Nature and Destiny of Man*, vol. 2, *Human Destiny* (New York: Charles Scribner's Sons, 1943), 252.

A Turn to the Penultimate

Between the relations with friends and family whom we can love personally and the ordered, impersonal relations of a whole society, we come to recognize another set of relationships, in which our response to God's action on us locates us in relationships where we work together with others to create and maintain the penultimate goods on which we all depend. Communities, jobs, schools, cultural institutions, and, indeed, congregations and denominations form this intermediate social reality, where we come together partly out of necessity, partly out of shared commitments, and partly out of simple recognition of our shared humanity. Forming people for love under conditions of human finitude involves helping them to take these relationships seriously.

The work of Christian formation described in this chapter is not, in itself, a response to the polarization that divides our society today. We have considered some ways that today's political context might change the way that the church approaches its task, but we should not suppose that these adjustments will be enough to make our divisions disappear. Indeed, a frontal assault on the forces of polarization, exposing the evils they perpetuate and denouncing their self-interested motives, quickly begins to sound like the problem it is supposed to solve. But the church must be clear in its own thinking that the polarization that marks our divided society is incompatible with the theocentric stance that listens for the Word of God. Faith in God who enters human life in Jesus Christ has always had to compete with dualistic theologies that

view history as a struggle between the forces of good and
evil, and Saint Augustine's *Confessions* offers a compelling account of just how appealing the Manichaean tale of
cosmic polarization could be to a young Roman intellec-
tual struggling with the competing accounts of happiness
available in his society.* We all enjoy the prospect of
having our choices vindicated by our success, or by the
failure of our enemies. But what Christian faith offers is
the hope of transformation. Loving our enemies includes
the possibility of a reconciliation in which we will both be
changed. What it does not include is a polarized view of
reality that insists we must remain enemies.

Polarization, to put the matter bluntly, achieves its
purposes by giving ultimate significance to penultimate
goods. Nation, race, language, political ideology, or, indeed, religion becomes the source of meaning against
which everything must be measured, and precisely because these limited realities are not adequate to that
purpose, they make themselves ultimate by depriving
other things of significance. When a finite good becomes
ultimate, all the other relationships in our lives—family,
church, work, and culture—have value insofar as they
serve the nation, the race, the party—or whatever has
been made ultimate for present purposes. Otherwise,
they must be opposed.

We are familiar with these idolatrous distortions of
political realities from the history of twentieth-century
totalitarian regimes, and because we know this history,

---

* Augustine, *Confessions*, Oxford World's Classics (Oxford: Oxford University Press, 1998), 40–89.

we sometimes accuse those we hold responsible for to-day's polarization of harboring authoritarian tendencies. Insofar as we are, in fact, free to say those things on Twitter and post them on our blog pages, we both refute our own accusations and contribute to further polarization. The ironic truth is that polarized politics, in contrast to totalitarianism, depends on opposition. It is the continued existence of the other side that allows us to explain why we have not delivered what our false ultimates promise. If the other side went away, we would be forced to deal with pandemic diseases, economic downturns, educational shortcomings, and structural discrimination on their own terms, rather than as if they were part of some big lie that evil people have imposed on us. To put the matter in Bonhoeffer's terms, without polarization and false ultimates, we would be forced to take the penultimate seriously. Listening to the Word leads us to listen to the world.

Listening to the World

Listening to the Word of God makes us aware that we cannot simply adapt and adjust to the realities of a divided society. But especially in a society that is divided in the way ours is, the church's work of formation is about listening to the Word of God in a way that makes it possible for us to listen to one another. Along with the Word we hear in the words spoken on Sunday morning, we need to hear more from the people who are part of our lives beyond the church. Listening means listening to the others with whom we create and maintain the things that make ordinary life possible, even in a divided society. Listening to the Word leads to a different way of listening to the world and to a renewed understanding of the things we do together with others in our everyday lives. Listening to the world involves shifting attention from the questions that pretend to be big to smaller problems that are closer to our own experience. It means paying attention to what we and those around us know about how to accomplish something together.

A Circle of Responsibility

Asking how all things are related to God as the source of their being, order, and meaning thus requires us also to pay attention to how things as we experience them are related to each other. It takes little effort to repeat the words of the Nicene Creed that affirm that God is "maker of all things, visible and invisible," but more is involved in trying to see these distinct and sometimes conflicting realities as part of one created order that includes human dreams and stubborn realities, the world we build and the forces of nature, ourselves and our enemies. We may be inspired by a starry sky on a clear night, or by a photo from space that allows us to see the whole earth set against the vast emptiness that surrounds it, but it is often more difficult to see created order on a human scale that includes distances to be covered, tasks to be completed, and, of course, other people.

Nevertheless, that is the scale on which faith must be lived. Bonhoeffer's insight into the task of Christian formation was to see that it has to be undertaken in relation to the penultimate goods of ordinary life, rather than in rare moments of spiritual insight or in big ideas put forward by political leaders. In ordinary life, we relate to other people. We take on roles and duties toward them. Together, we form organizations and institutions, and we are related through corporations, cities, and societies to people we do not know and will never meet. As we saw in the previous chapter, these relationships quickly take us outside our community of formation and beyond intimate connections to family and friends into what I will call a *circle of responsibility*, where we engage in common tasks and create possibilities that could not exist without this web of connections. This sphere tends to grow over the course of a lifetime, as we master new tasks and enter into new relationships, and we can expand it deliberately by reaching out to new people and making voluntary commitments to shared efforts. Sometimes this is done for reasons we would call altruistic or disinterested, simply because we care about the people who cross our paths and the ventures that matter to them. But just as important, and probably more familiar, are the occasions when we deliberately extend our circle of responsibility because we need new relationships, colleagues, and resources to deal with the responsibilities we have already undertaken.

Often, though not always, what is at the center of these responsibilities is a job. In theological terms, we might better name it a *vocation* or calling, to cover those whose circle of responsibility is tied to caring for a family, building up their neighborhoods and communities, or providing comfort and companionship in hospitals, nursing homes, and other care facilities. For Christians, vocation is important because it is the place where we actively build those connections between God and the world by which we come to a personal understanding of our faith. We are called to our tasks because it is in these concrete details that we can begin to see all things in relation to God. Without this circle of responsibility, a theocentric view of reality would remain an abstraction, a phrase vaguely remembered from a Tuesday Bible study group or a passing reference in a Sunday sermon. Indeed, most of the opportunities to make these connections come while we are not immediately thinking about the theological implications. We have deadlines, budgets, and production quotas to meet. We have a doctor's appointment for the baby and a parents' group that is meeting with the elementary school principal. We have promises to keep, choices to make, and a departmental "mission statement" tacked to the bulletin board to consider. These are the things that will occupy most of our attention.

Still, it makes sense to understand the results of these efforts in moral and theological terms. They are "goods." By that we mean not just material goods, such as furniture or face masks, nor even economic "goods and services" offered on the market, but "penultimate goods" in Bonhoeffer's sense, goals sought because they make human use of the good given in God's creation (Genesis 1:26–31).* Penultimate goods are what connect things within our circle of responsibility to the meaning they have in relation to God. Most of us are happy to take home a paycheck, but if we think about it in terms of our life of faith, much of the satisfaction we gain from work derives from a conviction that what we do meets real human needs. Pharmaceuticals and bed linens go to a hospital that provides a setting for the work of doctors and nurses, and that particular organization functions as part of a larger social structure of insurance, incentives, and regulation that makes health care affordable and widely available. Or at least it is supposed to. That is what we think we are doing

---

* Dietrich Bonhoeffer, *Ethics*, Dietrich Bonhoeffer Works, vol. 6 (Minneapolis: Fortress, 2005), 163. See above, pp. 61–65.

when we work at a calling. One aspect of our circle of responsibility, then, is that it is where we develop a detailed knowledge of how penultimate goods are created and an understanding of the institutions and social structures by which they are maintained.

Bonhoeffer's ethics alerts us to the theological significance of these penultimate goods, but ethical reflection on the ways they are created and maintained is ancient. Aristotle, who gave us the first systematic text on ethics in Western philosophy, begins, "Every art and every inquiry, and similarly every action and choice, is thought to aim at some good."* Taking time for such reflection on the goal of our activity can, of course, be seen as a kind of luxury, a leisure activity that those who grow the grain and bake the bread cannot afford. Aristotle may have been supported in his philosophical pursuits by good farm management on the part of those who cared for an estate in Macedonia that he had inherited from his father.** As a result, he was able to organize his thinking about human goods and virtues without paying much attention to the work of ordinary artisans or the virtues that might be found among farmers, slaves, and housekeepers. He seems to have thought that most people would do well enough by sticking to their craft and doing as they were told.

This attitude is still present in the modern world, where, only partly in jest, we warn people against taking on questions that are "above their pay grade." Indeed, we of-

---

* Aristotle, *Nicomachean Ethics* 1094a (trans. W. D. Ross).

** See a review of surviving evidence in Carlo Natali, *Aristotle: His Life and School* (Princeton: Princeton University Press, 2013), 7–10.

ten impose a sort of servitude on ourselves by concentrat-
ing on the specialized knowledge necessary to our tasks.
This enables us to produce complex goods, for which we
may be highly compensated, while avoiding questions
about any larger good of which they are a part.

For people of faith, however, a circle of responsibility
is more than a way to earn a living. It is a place to listen to
the world in ways that both learn from and contribute to
the ways we listen to the Word. The complex structures
in which human goods are related to one another mirror
the complex ways that faith understands them related to
God.* Taking these goods seriously also relates us in important ways to other people, even when they do not share
our faith. Precisely because all are part of this world of
God's creation, no one is excluded from living the moral
life that Aristotle described, no matter what Aristotle
thought about the philosophical capabilities of ordinary
human beings. When people recognize in each other real
concerns for penultimate things, it builds mutual respect
and increases cooperation among them. As they begin to
understand how other people live and the complex questions that are part of their daily lives, they recognize that
everyone has something to contribute to shared questions
that we face together. They do not view anyone who is
different as being self-interested or simply evil, and so
they are less likely to turn to false ultimates and polarized
identities to explain their problems.

---

* See the extended discussion of human capacities and responsibilities in God's creation in Douglas F. Ottati, *A Theology for the
Twenty-First Century* (Grand Rapids: Eerdmans, 2020), 249–68.

That is not to say that this mutual respect is free of conflict. Real goods are really different from one another, which means that understanding how they are related will also involve choices between them. Freedom and order are goods, but we cannot usually have all we want of both, either in the office or in society. Affordable and available medical care is a complex good, as we just noted, but so is the creation, preservation, and presentation of works of art. Within penultimate limits of time and resources, such goods may be in competition, and part of the task of creating and maintaining concrete goods is making a case for them in this competition.

Like the goods themselves, the considerations by which we make choices between them are complex and balanced, and the work of creating and maintaining goods often moves too fast to explain it in detail. Legal structures, organization charts, and market mechanisms do a great deal of the work for us, day to day. But when we ask ourselves why we do what we do, when we share those reflections with those who work with us, and when we try to persuade others to join us in creating the goods for which we are responsible, we do not simply settle for market price as a measure of meaning. Nor do we restrict ourselves to a "thin" theory of the good that dissolves what is distinctive about the goods we create into a few generic goods on which everyone can agree. And even if we acknowledge that it is difficult to explain how we would choose—if it comes to that—between the highest values such as beauty, freedom, equality, and excellence, we do not easily give in to "value pluralism" that says there are no shared reasons we could give for that kind of choice. Part of recognizing that goods are genuinely different from one another is giving reasons when we have to choose between them, even when the good we choose against has very strong claims of its own.

Virtues

Our moral lives consist largely of the choices we make between these competing penultimate goods. Sometimes these are large choices that shape our future, as when we decide on a career, or pursue education that gives us a new set of skills and a different perspective on our circle of responsibility. Sometimes the choices are urgent and conflicted. We may decide that it is time to raise questions about the social consequences of the way our company does business, or we might find ourselves in the position of the "whistleblower" who exposes deceptive and possibly dangerous shortcuts. But most often, we create and maintain the goods we have chosen by the daily decisions that get things done—effectively, efficiently, and with respect for the people around us. In this way, we do more than create penultimate goods. We form ourselves and others as persons.

Most of us could not easily say how we make these complex choices. We might recall how we made some of the important personal choices that put us where we find ourselves, or we might look back with regret on specific failures, but our ordinary choices come too fast for that kind of reflection. The complex relationships that make up the goods we seek are best seen in the habits and dis-

positions that shape our actions. Living in a circle of responsibility, we learn to see how things are connected. We
become habituated to the decisions our responsibilities
require, and we develop skills that get the work done and
draw others into collaboration with us. Over time, as we
learn more about the goods that are the goal of our actions, people around us recognize these habits and dispositions, and we recognize them in others. "She's a good
engineer" or "he's a good teacher" says as much about
the person as it does about the bridges she designs or the
test scores his pupils achieve.

The general term for these habits and dispositions is
virtue.* Like the theological virtues of faith, hope, and
love through which we understand our relationship to God,
these practical or moral virtues guide our interactions with
the world and other people. Some of them are so closely
tied to specific circles of responsibility that we do not even
have names for them. What do you call the disposition that
enables a physician to put a new patient immediately at
ease and quickly elicit an honest account of symptoms and
lifestyle? What are the habits by which a good manager
consistently both encourages teamwork and maintains
individual accountability? But we also generalize these
habits across different circles, and for some of these generalizations, old terms fit nicely: A person shows "prudence"

---

* Aristotle called such a disposition an *aretē*, or excellence. Acquiring and exercising these excellences make one a good person,
just as excellence in medicine or gymnastics makes a good physician or athlete. Our English word *virtue* has the disadvantage of
being too narrowly associated with moral goodness, along with the
problem that its origin in the Latin word *vir* (man) subtly suggests
that only males can show us what good character means.

in carefully choosing appropriate means to a good end. Someone is "just" or "fair" if they treat others equally and only make distinctions between them for good reasons. A "courageous" person persists toward good goals, even when there are obstacles to be overcome and risks involved, though obviously the courage of an emergency first responder is different from the courage of a teacher who works with developmentally challenged students.

Partly because our language for these virtues is very general and somewhat dated, we often fail to use these terms to connect the goods we seek and the personal characteristics that allow us to achieve them. We focus on results and ignore the people who make goods possible. We discount the extent to which our goals both depend on and are shaped by these aspects of our character. We may even think of virtue as a kind of rigid moral rectitude that gets in the way of what we want to achieve, rather than as a way of thinking and acting that makes the achievements possible. Simply put, the ordinary virtues that often go unnamed are the habits through which our knowledge of human goods becomes effective and active. By paying attention to the complex relationships between things and between persons that make human goods possible, we arrive at the choices that shape our circle of responsibility, and through creating and maintaining these human goods that we share, we become good persons.

Formation

In chapter 3, when we were focused on listening to the Word, we discussed "formation" in connection with the ways that the church shapes spiritual life, helping people express the theological virtues of faith, hope, and love. But the idea of formation also has a long history in relation to practical virtues like prudence, courage, and justice. Formation is how we acquire the many ordinary virtues that shape daily life within our circles of responsibility. Earlier in our history, education included explicit attention to this moral formation, with texts and lessons designed to produce habits of moral judgment and conscientious citizenship along with readiness for the world of work.

This kind of formation still takes place, though in today's world we are often too focused on immediate results to notice it. That is part of why the language of virtue seems old-fashioned. We are still acquiring virtues, but we are no longer naming them. Our workplaces largely require us to finish the job, follow the rules, and file the appropriate reports to show that we did. This is true, incidentally, for those of us whose circle of responsibility is in the classroom and whose job is to teach ethics.

In addition, diverse backgrounds, beliefs, and commitments make it hard to find a common language in which to talk about formation. Can we talk about justice, courage, or respect when we are trying to deal with race, the environment, or human sexuality? Can we do it without appealing to religious beliefs or other values that may not be shared? Will someone who raises these questions be perceived as disruptive just for bringing them up? In our divided society, even mentioning a social issue may identify you with a polarized opinion about it, so we avoid raising problems that require moral discussions, except when we know that everybody in the room already agrees with us.

But formation in virtue is still necessary, even if present conditions largely require us to hold conversations about it in an internal dialogue with ourselves. Our focus on immediate questions and our divisions over important social issues result in a shrinking public moral vocabulary, so that we discover that we do not know how to raise the questions, even when we think they are urgent and important for everyone around us. Without the kind of formation that turns our ways of working into practical virtues and allows us to recognize them in others around us, doing good work deteriorates into strategies for self-promotion, and our circle of responsibility shrinks until it becomes indistinguishable from self-interest.

Despite these contemporary limitations, Christian theology has a long history of concern with vocation and with formation in practical virtues. A theocentric spirituality that listens to the Word and relates all things to God becomes a series of empty platitudes unless it is accompanied by a sense of responsibility that recognizes that "God is acting in all actions upon you. So respond to all actions upon you as to respond to his action."[*] Singing praises to the "immortal, invisible, God only wise" lacks spiritual substance unless we remember that to love God, whom we have not seen, we must love our neighbors, whom we can see (1 John 4:20). A theocentric understanding begins with the recognition that difficult people and intractable problems that show up in our lives are also part of God's creation and must be understood in relation to God's pur-

---

[*] H. Richard Niebuhr, *The Responsible Self* (New York: Harper & Row, 1963), p. 126. See above, pp. 83–84.

poses. For Christians, moral virtues like honesty, fairness, and compassion are part of a theocentric understanding, quite as much as faith, hope, and love.

In addition to this enduring theology of vocation, the shrinking moral vocabulary available in our public life today leaves the church with an important social mission to provide opportunities for reflection on vocation that are largely missing from other settings, including the places where we actually work at those callings. Many people in our congregations have questions about their work and their workplaces, but do not know how to share them there. Precisely because that experience is so common in our divided society, the church might provide a place for talking about these issues, even among people whose actual vocational experiences are quite different from one another. They are seeking to respond, as to God's action, to all sorts of difficult, troubling realities, and they may not even have words to name what they feel called to do.

Unfortunately, opportunities to discuss these vocational and social issues in a church setting are not as common as the steady stream of social pronouncements by denominational agencies and the proliferation of ethics courses in theological seminaries might lead us to expect. Clergy find it difficult to venture beyond their own vocational expertise, and it is easier to sing another hymn than to devote a few minutes of the sermon to a controversy in the local school board that is on a lot of minds in the congregation or to a debate in Congress that has been covered in all the news media during the past week. The problem is compounded by the fact that those in the pews have often chosen, consciously or unconsciously, to be there because they are comfortable with the opinions they think others sitting alongside them share. Better, perhaps, not to open a discussion that might reveal divisions. Moreover, asking people to talk to other church members about problems in the places where they work or serve lacks the reality check that is provided when the discussion takes place among those who actually do share the same circle of responsibility. These are significant limitations, but they can be overcome if a congregation is willing to undertake this essential part of moral formation.

In most cases, this should begin in small-group discussions that provide opportunities for people to talk about their own experience and encourage the participants to ask questions that may help someone understand what they have been waiting for a chance to say. Participants may think that they are waiting for someone to explain to them what a Christian vocation is, but it would be a mistake to rely too much on clergy expertise. The task is to give space for both shared experiences and genuine differences to emerge. A developed theology of vocation will be useful at points,* but it may be better to introduce elements of it when it seems appropriate to the discussion, rather than to set it out systematically. Experienced pastors are good at quickly providing content when it is diffi-

---

* See, for example, Ottati, *Theology for the Twenty-First Century*, 622-39; Douglas Schuurman, *Vocation: Discerning Our Callings in Life* (Grand Rapids: Eerdmans, 2004); William C. Placher, *Twenty Centuries of Christian Wisdom on Vocation* (Grand Rapids: Eerdmans, 2005); Gustaf Wingren, *Luther on Vocation* (Eugene, OR: Wipf & Stock, 2004); Alister McGrath, "Calvin and the Christian Calling," *First Things* 94 (June/July 1999): 31-35.

cult to get a discussion going, but this subject may require a slower start than others. Certainly, the best sermons on vocation are the ones written after these discussions, not the ones brought in to structure them from the outset.

If the discussion itself needs to be honest and spontaneous, advance planning can compensate for the limits of vocational diversity in a congregation or make use of its particular strengths. Insulation from those who share the same work may help participants to be more honest with themselves. Explaining to others why they do what they do at work may help them see things that they had not noticed about their vocational culture. Alternatively, a large congregation may be able to gather small groups who share a professional background in medicine, law, or education and who will benefit from thinking about their work in relation to their faith with others who have had similar experiences. A congregation with many "front-line" workers can provide important opportunities for them to talk about how they see their responsibilities to the people they serve. In those relationships, they share concerns that cut across the differences between their lines of work, and their priorities may be different from those of their employers or supervisors. A hospital aide, a mail carrier, and a grocery checkout clerk who each see their work as a vocation may find they have a lot in common if they happen to be part of a congregation that gives them a chance to talk about it.

Equally important, congregations that lack vocational diversity in their own membership are often involved in denominational groups, community organizations, and councils of churches that provide remarkable exposure to a wide range of people and communities. Regular meetings, short-term study groups, and special events all can provide settings for a focus on questions about work and society, but interaction between different participants in a service project, a food pantry, or a fundraiser has real value for learning how other people listen to the world, quite apart from the good that the project was designed to achieve. In a divided society where people have few opportunities to venture beyond the places where others generally share their experiences and their opinions, congregations have unusual opportunities to encourage their members to take a new look at their circles of responsibility, if they understand that kind of listening as part of the task of Christian formation.

Many of these activities that connect people across our usual lines of division are commonly seen as church activities, and people often seek out a congregation or a fellowship group precisely because it provides these opportunities. They are thus part of evangelism and outreach, but it is important to resist the temptation to "brand" them as specific to the church. The goal of formation is for Christians to carry what they learn through the church into the rest of their lives and act on it there. Formation becomes effective when it is lived in ways that other people can understand and incorporate into their actions, even if they do not share the same faith. In a society where Christian faith has to compete with a range of consumer identities, churches and clergy have an understandable urge to stress their unique contributions by providing a distinctly "Christian" understanding of vocation and assuring everyone that the best evidence of authentic

Christianity is that it is incomprehensible to those who do not share their faith and their vocabulary. But this is no help to those trying to live a theocentric faith in relation to the goods they help to create and to the virtues they bring to their vocations. They will be seeking a language of penultimate goods that can be widely shared and that grows out of their common experience with others who share similar responsibilities. There is a theological task in those vocations, but in our divided society, that task is chiefly to draw people away from the false ultimates that a polarized worldview offers and refocus attention on specific problems that we can solve together.

Penultimate Politics

If our consumer identities make it difficult to connect Christian faith with a circle of responsibility, our divided society makes it equally difficult to relate politics to penultimate goods. Our circle of responsibility is a familiar place where we connect with people with whom we have to cooperate every day. Especially in these polarized times, it seems best to keep politics out of it, even in the break room or around the water cooler, assuming that our workplace still has break rooms and water coolers. Politics happens somewhere else. We access politics online, and we connect to it through well-known commentators who tell us about it from a perspective that we have come to expect. We see politics through the lens of Fox News or PBS, but the scale is always large, even when the screen is small. Politics gathers up the things to be done into big packages that involve trillions of dollars, and today, especially, politics asks us to choose one of those big packages as the ultimate goal. Everything we need is in that package, and the quickest way to understand the alternatives is that the other package is everything that we do not want. We are necessarily more realistic about our circles of responsibility, which connect us to limited goods and local institutions. Politics is a break from the pressure of these responsibilities, a rally where we get a chance to cheer for a package of ultimate goods. We may even get a T-shirt that reduces it all to a logo so that others will know what we stand for, or just in case we have difficulty figuring that out ourselves.

At the beginning of our history of thinking about these questions, however, "politics" meant something more like what goes in the places where people create the common goods that sustain a way of life for themselves and for others. Then, too, there were famous orators who whipped up the crowds at public assemblies. There were generals who led their armies into battle and always came back claiming victory. There were kings who wore crowns and ordinary people who were taught that they should stick to their tasks and not think too much about things that were over their heads. Those ordinary people probably made up most of the crowds who came out to hear Jesus, and he seems to have enjoyed teasing them for their fascination with wealth and power. "What then did you go out to see?" he asked the crowds who went out to the wilderness in search of John the Baptist. "Someone dressed in soft robes? Look, those who put on fine clothing and live in luxury are in royal palaces" (Luke 7:25).

He could draw them into his parables by inviting them to imagine themselves as rich landowners ordering their servants about or handing out rewards to stewards who looked after their property (Luke 17:7–10; 19:12–27). His point, of course, was to contrast the way God really works in their world with their fantasies about the lifestyles of the rich and famous.

Jesus's teaching was radical in this respect, certainly compared to Aristotle, who seems to have taught that the goods worth thinking about were those that could be pursued by a leisured elite. But even Aristotle tried to ground political thinking in virtues, rather than in a search for power. The work that we call Aristotle's *Ethics* introduces the subject with terms that translate closer to "politics" or "political science," because it is a study of the goods and virtues that make a city—a *polis*—possible.* Politics is about what holds a human community together. Politics enables them to create the goods on which they all depend and forms their virtues in such a way that when they create a city, they are also able to live a good life.

Politics understood in this way begins with human goods and virtues on a personal level and expands step-by-step as these people join with others to create a whole complex of goods and the institutions to maintain them. The good workshop, school, theater, and market in turn make up a city that requires specifically political structures to maintain its peace, order, and security. If the scale of these structures was at first small, we can recognize in

---

* Aristotle, *Nicomachean Ethics* 1095a. The Greek word is *politikē*.

the Greek city-states that Aristotle described the origins of many of the institutions we still depend on, and if the work of peace and order fell at first to heads of clans and prestigious individuals, it quickly evolved into a structure of government that was itself a penultimate good, no less than the structures of work and culture.

The direction of this development from the particular to the more general is important. Human goods do not become good when someone announces a program or a party platform that includes them. They are built from small things that become significant because people know how to make them and derive both satisfaction and their own sustenance from connecting them to the needs of others. Feeding the hungry, as Bonhoeffer might say, begins with knowing how to bake bread.* The right to health care begins with the work of healing, and with hospitals, clinics, and emergency services that organize the complex skills involved so that care can be delivered. A right to health care has no meaning without the multiple vocations that make health care possible, just as the best health care in the world cannot be a human good for those in a city who have no access to it. Law is a penultimate good that provides justice, community, and order,** but it begins with a practical knowledge of the structures of restraint and cooperation that make a neighborhood. Lawyers and police are little help where people do not know how to live together. Those who deliver groceries, prescriptions, and mail are often the people who under-

---

* See above, pp. 64–65.
** Bonhoeffer, *Ethics*, 163.

stand best how concrete goods can draw out the lonely and create community.

The politics of penultimate goods begins from the ground up. It happens as people take up responsibilities for goods that are within their reach and extend themselves toward others who need these goods, who have the resources that help to create and maintain them, or who connect them to other goods that are also required to make good lives possible. In these ways a community forms the virtues that are required for its own future. We are often painfully aware of our own inability to meet these responsibilities, or even angry at others who have, in quite specific ways, kept us from doing so. But the politics of penultimate goods does not assume that we already know everything there is to know about how to create the goods, structures, and systems we need and that if we fail, it is because large and evil forces are working against us. That excuse seems to work only on the large scale of polarized politics that we encounter at rallies, on social media, or in sound bites reported from Washington and the halls of our state legislatures.

This does not mean that there are no conflicts in a politics that begins from the ground up. The hard fact of human finitude is that we simply cannot have all we want of all the goods we want. Achieving any penultimate good requires the sacrifice of some others, from which we take the time and resources necessary to create and maintain the goods we have chosen. It would be more convenient if reality were polarized like our politics, so that we could have the goods we want by taking power and resources from those our leaders have told us not to trust. But reality is not polarized. To have particular goods, we must make sacrifices, and we must ask sacrifices from others who want different goods.*

Theocentric Faith and Penultimate Goods

We need to form Christians in the ordinary virtues that make cooperation possible, not only in a divided society, but in the realities of penultimate politics where we contend with one another for the goods that are most central to our own responsibilities. In the absence of faith, hope, and love, there may be little reason to suppose that collaboration is possible, except when it involves joining forces against somebody else who wants something different. A theocentric faith that relates all things to God as source, guide, and goal and responds to God's action in all actions on us will take us beyond what we can clearly see and beyond the polarized alternatives that political leaders set up for us. Today, even churches are drawn into creating consumer identities and adapting to polarized politics. Little wonder, then, that they have a hard time forming people whose ordinary, workaday virtues are also connected to the theological virtues of faith, hope, and love. That is why ideology and authoritarianism are drawing widespread support. It also explains why utopian appeals that promise to preserve the environment, share wealth, secure peace, and make all lives matter are initially so

* See the initial description of circles of responsibility on pp. 103–9 above.

attractive. It is easy to want the goods when no one talks about the costs. Above all, the hard work that real responsibilities demand explains why anger and resentment are never far below the surface, even in penultimate politics. It is easier to blame someone else for our failures than to love our enemies, have faith in redemption, and hope for reconciliation. Polarization offers an easy and false solution to all of these problems.

Theocentric faith enables us to value penultimate goods and see them in relation to ultimate reality. Indeed, it allows us to trust our own virtues, within limits, because those virtues are the ways of living and working by which we create the penultimate goods that are within reach in our circles of responsibility. At the same time, because this faith is centered in God, we can see the limits of our virtues and the goods we create. It is not necessary to conjure up other forces that are supposedly out to destroy them. Listening to the Word *and* listening to the world allow us to talk about politics in ways that recognize limits without drawing boundaries.

To sustain penultimate goods, we must find ways to draw other people into the work of creating them with us. Having any good involves choices, and making those choices last involves persuading other people to join in them. We might do this more easily if we had shared ways of talking about rights, duties, dignity, and equality in which to frame our arguments. But in a divided society, this shared moral vocabulary shrinks as each side claims more and more of the terms for itself.* Politicians, preachers, and professors of ethics will continue to work

* See above, pp. 26–27.

on rebuilding the terminology, but the work of politics at the level where political communities are built is going to depend more and more on being able to hear our neighbors' needs and hopes and build durable penultimate goods that provide something for all of us. It is important to keep talking about human rights, and voting rights, and freedom, and responsibility, and sustainability. But in a divided society where somebody else already owns most of those terms, the most effective political argument for any good is finding people who will actually join with us to create it.

Listening to Those Who Are Not Heard

Our divided society encourages a dualistic worldview. Political parties, candidates and elected leaders, nations, policies, and individual persons are divided into two opposing sides, each of which sees the other as the main obstacle to its aspirations. *They* are devoted to goods that are at odds with the goods we seek. Or perhaps they have no good apart from their own self-interest. Or maybe they are a tiny core group of evildoers, and they have deceived a gullible following into opposing *us*. A certain looseness in the definition of the other side is essential. Whoever they are, and whatever it is that they believe, they are resisting and opposing what we already know is good. The important thing is not to listen to them, we are told, so that we can give full attention to the real facts that our side has uncovered. Thus, a divided society reduces our ability to hear anything new at the same time that it bombards us with more and more messages that we have already heard. Our email inboxes fill up with advice about what to do, be, think, buy, and donate to—all urgently requiring a response before 11 p.m. tonight.

Sending the message that your opponents are just about to ruin everything encourages people to pay attention to you, so that they will be prepared to defend themselves against the right, or the left, or the forces of lawlessness, or the forces of repression. But the forces of evil also provide an easy explanation for failure to deliver on our own promises. Politicians, pundits, opinion-makers, and media personalities do not need to deliver results or provide new ideas. They just need to maintain the opposition. Polarization may be hard to live with, but it thus proves to be a remarkably stable way to do politics. Intense loyalties are easy to provoke if there is someone to be against, and critical thinking—especially self-critical thinking—seems disloyal when there is so much at risk. Once the divisions are in place, it is easier to maintain them than to end them. The real risk is not that we will miss tonight's deadline, but that we become unable to hear anything that does not demand attention so insistently as to drown out any other messages. The people we most need to hear speak softly, when they are able to speak at all. Unless we are attuned to respond to them as a response to God's action on us, we will not be able to find a new way beyond the divisions that are now set so firmly in place. The church's work of formation that prepares us to listen to the Word and listen to the world must also form us to listen to those we do not hear.

Who Matters?

The dynamics of polarization do not encourage listening. Except when we are in a mood to stoke our indignation, we largely ignore the familiar slogans, the predictable results of investigations into what the other side is doing, and the eloquent press briefings offered by our own standard bearers just in time for the network news. But the problem is more basic than mere repetition. Polarization maintains itself by grabbing anything that is new and quickly assigning it a place in the order of things—red or blue, progressive or conservative, socialist or free market, anarchy or order, insurrection or the rule of law.

It is hardly surprising, then, that when the murder of George Floyd occurred during a volatile campaign season in the summer of 2020, the assertion that "Black Lives Matter" became a matter of partisan politics. What we might have learned from particular Black voices, what people in the streets thought would matter in their own communities, what people were already trying to do that might make a difference to these specific problems—all that quickly gave way to the urgent business of assigning blame to the people we were already blaming for everything else. To be sure, much hard work was done in local communities—some of it by churches. Those efforts may yet bear fruit in new understandings and changed practices. But the political institutions and movements that have these questions most immediately in their circles of responsibility were largely unable to do more than assimilate the events into the polarized worldviews they already held.

A similar dynamic played out during the COVID-19 pandemic, when scientific research and public health mandates were seldom discussed on their own terms. Instead, the public debate moved almost immediately to long-standing issues of individual freedom versus social responsibility, and policy choices were dictated more by the need to take a stand than by evidence about outcomes. Things might have been different if the questions of fact had been easier or if the political situation had been less volatile, but in its broad outlines this case, too, illustrates the way that polarization maintains a curious version of political stability by casting everything in terms of oppositions that are always a crisis, but never come to an end. What polarization requires, with its intense loyalties and shortage of critical thinking, is that people who raise different questions are not heard.

Christians who are formed by listening to the Word should, however, be alert to people whom their society overlooks. Moral and religious authorities, ancient and modern, have sometimes held rather narrow views about whose voices should be heard and whose lives deserve to be considered. By contrast, Jesus in the Gospels consistently draws attention to those who have gone unnoticed and unheard. His stories and parables address many different themes, but always this attention to those we do not hear is included in their meaning. Lazarus, the beggar at the gate who lives on scraps from the rich man's table, finds himself in paradise with Abraham. The rich man, whom we usually call Dives, who was so important in his lifetime, is not even named (Luke 16:19–31).* Mary gets a place along with the men listening to Jesus, and probably asking questions, too (Luke 10:38–42). A poor widow who lacks the means to make a show of her piety is said to

---

* "Dives" simply means "rich man" in Latin.

make the largest gift in a crowd of worshipers (Luke 21:1–4). Jesus, however, refused to be drawn into the legal arguments between Pharisees and Herodians over whether to pay taxes to Caesar or the theological disputes between the Pharisees and the Sadducees (Mark 12:13–27). Perhaps then as now, opposing sides in polarized arguments kept the disputes going to maintain their own authority.*

The disciples of Jesus not only remembered the examples he set out. They tried to follow them. Paul turned the disputes between Pharisees and Sadducees to his advantage when forced to defend himself in Jerusalem (Acts 23:6–9), and Christian communities that heard the Spirit speaking through both Jews and Greeks held an ideal of unity and equality in Christ, even if they did not always realize it in practice (Galatians 3:28). In contrast to religious movements that drew distinctions between themselves and others, or within the group between those who had "knowledge" and those who did not, the early church grew by taking in those whom others excluded and enlisting them to extend it still wider (2 Corinthians 10:13–18).

We could spend considerable time on historical and sociological studies that trace the rapid expansion of Christianity eastward and westward from its origins around Jerusalem, determine who exactly these people were who had gone unheard, and identify parallels between their situation in the ancient world and the marginalized groups in our own.** We could certainly develop more fully the ways

---

* I owe this interpretation to Rev. Sophia Hyon, from a sermon she preached at First United Methodist Church in Chicago.

** The background and history of early Christianity are comprehensively examined in parts 1–3 of Diarmaid McCulloch, *Christianity: The First Three Thousand Years* (New York: Viking, 2010).

in which important moral systems that we have inherited from that world, like Aristotle's account of goods and virtues, allow us to avoid listening to the people on whom our opportunities for reflection depend. We could even trace the ways in which the church through history has passed over without notice the central place that Jesus gave to those on the margins of society.

Instead, Howard Thurman's classic study *Jesus and the Disinherited* asks us to consider "what the teachings and the life of Jesus have to say to those who stand . . . with their backs against the wall."* What we learn from that perspective underlines how seeing the origin and end of all things in God and responding to the world as a response to God's action on us differs from ways of thinking that create identity by giving ultimate meaning to distinctions that separate us from others. Polarization is a modern development, dependent on wide participation in politics, instant communications, and a certain tendency to turn our leaders into popular icons; but the human propensity to simplify the world by deciding that there are some people we do not need to hear has been at odds with listening to the Word for a long time.

Responsiveness and Responsibility

The crucial question, however, is, "Who are we not hearing *now*?" If we are responsive to God in all reality, we cannot

---

A sociological account is provided by Rodney Stark, *The Rise of Christianity* (Princeton: Princeton University Press, 1996).

* Howard Thurman, *Jesus and the Disinherited* (Boston: Beacon, 1996), 11.

listen selectively, according to our own criteria for what is worth hearing. But neither can we listen to the whole world at once. The kind of listening that might change who we hear begins in our circles of responsibility.

We hear those who are not heard by enlarging our circle of responsibility to include those who are at the edges of the work we do and the lives we live, the people we too quickly assume are irrelevant to what we are trying to accomplish. We also need to include those just beyond the limits of our responsibilities, who might make a difference if we heard them and understood how they are connected to the human goods with which we are concerned.

To include someone in our circle of responsibility is not the same thing as *taking responsibility for* them. That quickly reverts to the model of ethics that assumes that other people will do well if they do what we tell them to do. Nor is it a matter of trying to make them *be responsible*, as though the world would be a better place if everyone just took care of themselves and did not trouble others about it. We all spend a certain amount of time just trying to get the books in order and the laundry done without interruptions, but the important goods we try to create and maintain are not simply arrangements we make for ourselves. What makes our daily life meaningful is that we are responsible for penultimate goods that meet common human needs and make a good life possible for everyone. We do not find out what these goods are and how to make them more secure by protecting them from other people. We learn that by enlisting more people in what we hope to accomplish, figuring out how the goods that concern us are connected to the goods for which they are responsible, and identifying the distinctive virtues that they can bring to bear on our common tasks.

At this moment in our history, this will not be a matter of finding arguments on which we can all agree. That may be how moral reasoning should work, but in a divided society each side begins with the assumption that it already owns the moral arguments. Attempts at persuasion often end with each side thinking it has not been heard by the other and perhaps deciding that it will not be worth listening in the future. As we noted at the end of the previous chapter, in a divided society, the best way to make an argument for any good is actually to create it. Doing that requires us to be more responsive. We expand our circle of responsibility by bringing more people into creating and maintaining the penultimate goods for which we are responsible. In so doing, we become part of their circles of responsibility, too. When we pay attention to what we can do together, we discover who it is that we do not hear.

The Many Whom We Do Not Hear

Some of those who go unheard are truly marginalized and may have difficulty speaking for themselves. People without homes who live in extreme poverty, who are perhaps mentally ill, and whom circumstances have rendered unable to care for themselves or others have a special need for the penultimate goods of food, shelter, and protection. These are among the people of whom Jesus took notice. Their needs have been a particular concern of the church from the beginning, and many Christians find their circle of responsibility in meeting those needs. Those who do that quickly learn that even here there is listening to be done—a story to be heard in exchange for a sandwich, or flashes of wit and moments of compassion from people who appear largely disconnected from their surroundings. It is important to listen to them and not just to help them, and though we must recognize extreme poverty when we see it, we must be careful not to create a world of poor people whom we have to help according to our ideas of what they need.

In any case, the number of truly marginalized people we encounter is, for most of us, very small compared to the number of people we do not hear simply because we are not listening. We often find them, when we take care to look, right in the middle of our daily life. The brusque doctor who seems to have little time for the patients at the community clinic where we volunteer turns out to have a compelling story to tell when he speaks to the agencies that fund it, and he is an effective recruiter of medical colleagues who participate in the work. The woman who slips in and out to fix computers in the office or delivers mail and packages without a word may prove to be a formidable presence in her church or her neighborhood association. We will probably never truly listen to more than a fraction of these people with whom we interact, but when we take a moment to ask whose voices we are not hearing, we recognize that it is usually our inattention, rather than something they lack, that causes them to go unheard.

Other forms of inattention that are harder to overcome are built into our consciousness by social forces that shape us before we are even aware of them. Because of structural racism, there are groups we rarely encounter in daily life. Yet we acquire strong expectations about what these people think and how they will behave based on appearances, even when they appear to us mostly on television screens and in the movies. Our minds assign social roles based on race and gender, and although we sometimes congratulate ourselves on being pleasantly surprised when we encounter an individual who transcends those expectations, we rarely challenge the underlying expectations or ask what we might do to change them. The social structures of caste are even more resistant because they give rise to expectations of deference and superiority that are shared on both sides. There are those we do not hear because we do not expect to hear from them, and there are those who will be silent because they have learned it is dangerous to speak up.*

So the world to which we listen is nonetheless crowded with people whom we do not hear. We see some of the reasons for this clearly enough when we pay attention to our own inattention. The social forces behind this failure to hear are harder to grasp, and it takes some effort to understand why ordinary social interactions often leave us quite clueless about what is happening with

---

* Structural racism is a problem because discriminatory results are built into institutions in ways that persist independently of racist attitudes. Distinctions of caste, as sociologists understand them, are receiving increased attention because they create identities and expectations in which all groups implicitly accept the prevailing assignments of superiority and inferiority. See Isabel Wilkerson, *Caste: The Origins of Our Discontents* (New York: Random House, 2020).

other people involved. Beyond our personal biases and limitations, which we can recognize when we are honest with ourselves, the explanations of how race, class, caste, and power divide us are complex, and even after we grasp them intellectually, it may be difficult to see them at work in our own experience. For some, these theories seem to be just another example of special interests making an argument for their own purposes. What started as an explanation of the social conditions that some people experience is seen by other people as a way to blame them for the problems. Like many other things in our divided society, the explanations of our divisions have themselves become polarized.*

Pushing the Boundaries

We can learn much from these theoretical accounts of social structures and hierarchies, but unless your circle of responsibility involves ethics or sociology, it may be more relevant to ask how to change how people are heard in the institutions with which you are directly involved.

---

* State legislatures have debated whether public schools should teach "critical race theory" and other accounts of structural racism. Trip Gabriel and Dana Goldstein, "Disputing Racism's Reach, Republicans Rattle American Schools," *New York Times*, June 1, 2021, https://www.nytimes.com/2021/06/01/us/politics/critical-race -theory.html; Arian Campo-Flores, Joshua Jamerson, and Douglas Belkin, "On the Anniversary of George Floyd's Killing, Debate about Race Reaches across American Life," *Wall Street Journal*, May 25, 2021, https://www.wsj.com/articles/george-floyd-death -anniversary-11621912455?st=ez22omhrsynjeli.

How would the specific penultimate goods that occupy our time and energy every day be different if we made them more available to the people we do not hear? What skills and virtues that we do not have might they bring to creating and maintaining these goods, and how would our virtues have to change to include theirs?

These questions are especially important to community organizations, clubs and groups that form around shared activities, and cultural institutions like museums and performance groups that provide shared opportunities for learning and enjoyment. Churches, too, have an important role in this penultimate good of community, as anybody can see by looking at the calendar of events that happen in the building occupied by a vital congregation. The sociologist Robert Putnam has documented how participation in these shared activities has declined, with the result that we are now "bowling alone" instead of in a bowling league, if indeed we participate in organized recreation at all. The result, Putnam says, is not just a change in individual lives, but an enormous loss of the "social capital" needed to support inclusive organizations and livable communities.*

It should not escape our attention that the political polarization of our whole society followed on this loss of social capital in local communities. Whether the loss of social capital caused the polarization, allowed it to happen, or simply preceded it is, again, a question for sociological investigation. The important task now is constructing new

* Robert Putnam, *Bowling Alone: The Collapse and Revival of American Community*, rev. ed. (New York: Simon & Schuster, 2020).

associational loyalties at the local level. But replenishing our social capital cannot mean simply rebuilding communities along lines familiar from times past. "Social capital" also funded practices of discrimination and exclusion that set the stage for later social conflict. To address the problems of a divided society, we must also work to make sure that new opportunities reach across the ethnic, racial, religious, and neighborhood lines that marked out the patterns of association that we have lost.

Churches have an important role here, because they have connections that can reach across those lines and provide opportunities for people to work together and listen to each other in ways that do not happen if we rely only on the connections that are built in work and family life. Churches can help expand circles of responsibility by creating new connections, so that the participants listen to new people and enter new relationships. Again, this will not work if church activists simply try to take responsibility *for* other people, but the recognition of specific goods that a wider community can create together and work together to maintain provides a focus for really listening to everyone who is involved.

It may be more difficult to break with familiar patterns of listening and not listening in the circles of responsibility where we earn a living. While other forms of association have disappeared or been transformed into consumer identities, the world of work demands more and more of our time and energy, and the expectations seem to become more narrowly economic. Everything comes down to the bottom line. In that environment, listening may, in fact, be discouraged, especially if it means listening to people outside the familiar chain of command and involves communication about topics not on the agenda.

Yet even these inflexible requirements may yield to current events. The COVID-19 pandemic, the economic dislocations it caused, and the racial tensions that flared during the same time will require many changes, and unlike the disappearance of bowling leagues and community organizations, most of these changes will be felt in the world of work. Team members who have worked at home for many months will need to rethink how—and whether—they will return to working in the same space. Frontline workers who deal directly with the public have a new awareness of both their own vulnerability and the way their employers are dependent on them. Shops and suppliers whose customer base has changed will need to listen to new voices to rebuild their businesses, and in every store and office there is a new awareness of surrounding communities where needs and resentments have to be heard and understood.

The settings vary, but these expanding circles of responsibility share some common features. First, the work happens locally. National media may highlight the fact that there are similar problems everywhere, and public figures may describe them as national problems, but the changes must be tailored to local situations and relationships must be built between people who can be in regular contact with one another. The drive to be more inclusive can be measured demographically, but people have to work together on goods they need for statistical diversity to make a real difference.

Learning New Virtues

The church's work of formation should prepare its people for all these challenges. Listening to the world, as we saw in chapter 4, means understanding how people come together to create and maintain goods and identifying the virtues that enable them to do it. Those who are listening to the Word are at the same time learning to respond to the contending forces in our divided society as a response to God. They reach across boundaries to identify goods shaped even by people with whom they disagree, and they listen to how those people name the virtues that make their goods possible.

In a divided society, a lot of personal energy and social media attention goes into what is called "virtue signaling." We take care to use the correct terms for marginalized groups, including our own. We indicate our choice of pronouns to show we respect others' right to choose theirs. We make a point of using the colors, badges, and banners that show we know whose Heritage Month this is and that we are joining the celebration. All those signals are important and contribute to an atmosphere of inclusion. But often the message they send is more about us than about the people they are meant to respect. What we need is not "virtue signaling" but "virtue detection." That is, we need to understand the world of those whom we do not hear and learn the virtues that make that world work for them.

This is not simply a matter of recognizing those who have virtues we already know about, though given our stereotypes of class and caste, that may be difficult enough.

When we do not really listen to the people whose goods are at risk, their courage may look to us like cunning, and prudence may be scorned as submissiveness. We need to learn when the virtues we think we know are deployed in different ways, to maintain goods that are at risk from threats we do not understand. We need to be especially alert for situations when those virtues are being used against us. When we see what looks like cunning or deceit, it is worth asking what strength of character might lie behind it and what goods might lead someone to run those risks. When we take submissiveness to be a sign of weakness, we might consider whether we pose a threat that makes it prudent to end the confrontation and save the conflict for another day. The virtues we respect and seek to form in ourselves will not always be deployed by others for the same purposes for which we use them. Listening to those who are not heard involves recognizing courage, patience, humility, and claims to justice in their lives and asking what they seek to protect by these virtues.

What is more difficult, perhaps, is detecting the virtues we do not know, the habits and dispositions for which we have no names, though they hold the world together for those who practice them. The theologian Katie Geneva Cannon (1950–2018) studied the habits and dispositions by which Black women gain control of precarious situations by learning "what to say to the lion when your head is in the lion's mouth."* Cannon followed Alice Walker in

---

* Cannon credits her mother for this proverb. See Katie Geneva Cannon, *Katie's Canon: Womanism and the Soul of the Black Community* (New York: Continuum, 1995), 91–105.

naming this virtue "unctuousness." The name might be unappealing to people who are used to more control over their lives, but unctuousness empowers people who have the virtue to slip out of difficult situations with just the right amount of believable flattery and feigned humility. People who think they do not need this virtue may not pay attention to it, but in our overheated environment of social media attacks and public confrontations, it might be useful to a dean facing an angry group of "woke" faculty or a CEO with a dissatisfied board of directors.

The impulse to ignore or eliminate the virtues that work for other people shares something with Aristotle's aristocratic judgment that some skills are beneath moral notice. But in a divided society where important institutions are failing, it is worth noting how other people maintain their footing to accomplish their purposes, despite the dysfunction all around them. If we understand how other people get things done, we may find ways to work with them so that we share the goods that each other's virtues make possible.

Enlarging the Circles of Responsibility

This kind of listening is not easy. It leads to an active reassessment of our circles of responsibility, asking whether there are other ways of achieving the goods to which we are most committed and whether there are others who could join us in that effort. In our divided society, we are surrounded by warnings that it is dangerous to ask these questions. Goods have to be secured by protecting ourselves from those who threaten them, rather than by asking how to engage more people in creating them. Listening is what we do when we want to get something done. We send virtue signals when we want to be left alone.

That is not to say that larger communities are free from conflict. As we have noted before, real goods are really different from one another, so that creating and maintaining them always involves choices between them.* As more people who are committed to different goods become involved in the creation of any one of them, the number of choices to be made will increase, and more and different virtues will be needed to make those choices well. But as we make better choices in the creation of goods, the goods themselves become more secure and it is easier to maintain them. Instead of the defensive excuses of a divided society, we begin to build the structures of real politics, from the ground up.

If listening to the world builds circles of responsibility that understand penultimate goods, expanding those circles commits us to compromise and negotiation. Because we cannot have all we want of every good we want, having any of them requires understanding how they are related to other goods and collaborating with people who have different experiences and different commitments. That is what politics has required from the beginning, even if many of the people who wrote about politics had a restricted view of whose experiences and commitments deserve to be considered. If, today, "politicians" cannot make the compromises that politics requires, that may be

---

* See above, pp. 108–9.

because they have lost interest in political choices between competing goods and only want the power to choose.

In a society divided the way that ours is, Christians must resist temptations to adapt to polarization and find our own place within it. But neither can we respond by a strategy of withdrawal and resistance. In a world where no one is listening, no one will note our absence from the shouting, and we will simply be classified with one side or the other, as surely as if we had yielded to the temptation to choose one of them. Hearing the Word forms us for a theocentric faith in which all things and all people are related to God and thus related to us. If this is not apparent in the ways that we live together now, we are also formed to hope that we can make the unity of all things in God visible through our choices. That, however, will require us to enter the conflicts by which penultimate goods are created and maintained, for that is how love works within the conditions of finitude.*

* Reinhold Niebuhr, *The Nature and Destiny of Man*, vol. 2, *Human Destiny* (New York: Charles Scribner's Sons, 1943), 252. See above, p. 98.

Taking Up Space in a Divided Society

Through history, there have been many ways of thinking about the church in the wider society. Some theories stress the distinction between the church and the powers of government, while others make government subject to the laws of reason and nature as the church teaches them. Modern political thinkers treat the church as one among many voluntary organizations, while some contemporary theologians insist that the church must adopt a stance of resistance that sets it against every attempt that the rest of society makes to define its place. Some ways of thinking can hardly imagine a church apart from a Christian society, while others insist that the church is most free to be the church in a society that does not share its assumptions.

Dietrich Bonhoeffer knew these theories and used them to answer complex questions in his writings, but his most basic understanding of church and society was simple: The church of Jesus Christ "takes up space" in the world.* Whatever the surrounding culture, the relevant

---

* Dietrich Bonhoeffer, *Discipleship*, Dietrich Bonhoeffer Works, vol. 4 (Minneapolis: Fortress, 2001), 225. See above, pp. 39–45.

laws, or the church's theology may say, theocentric faith will make a difference in the ways that Christians relate to the world and to other people. Faith is not just a set of ideas they believe. Their lives are formed by it, and the world is changed by their presence in it. The world will know that Christians are there, whether or not the church has a theology or the world has a theory to explain the space they occupy.

Exactly how they occupy that space differs, of course, across nations, times, and cultures. Christians need to pay attention to how they make their presence known, especially in a divided society like ours, where claims about difference are loud and persistent. The church has always done things that make a difference in service, education, and spiritual formation, but it is important now to take up space in ways that challenge the expectations that polarize us.

Inclusiveness

In a divided society, the church takes up space by being inclusive. "All are welcome" is a way of life, not just a sign in rainbow colors at the church door—though the sign may be important in a world where many people have found church doors closed to them at points in their lives. Inclusiveness means giving people a voice as well as a seat at the table. It means reaching out, rather than waiting for them to show up, accommodating them in ways that enable them to participate, and recognizing that their history and culture are already a part of our past, as well as part of our future.

Inclusiveness thus takes up space within the church, and when it becomes part of the church's formation, Christians take up space. They ask how people are treated in the office, who gets recruited when the school needs volunteers, and where the boundary lines are drawn between "our" neighborhood association and "theirs," over there. All of these are risky behaviors, and they may create problems, both for the people who ask the questions and for those they were hoping to include. That is why Christian formation includes virtues by which we become effective, as well as urgent, in efforts toward change. Prudence tempers courage and justice overcomes mere indignation when it is the church that is taking up space, not just our own egos.

In a divided society, of course, inclusiveness may be just another way to consolidate one's own base and show how many of us there are in our new majority, against the dwindling and dispirited numbers on the other side. It is hard to tell from a group picture whether we are looking at a representative sample of those who already agree with us or a community that is genuinely inclusive.

The inclusiveness formed by theocentric faith, however, sees people in relationship to God and not just in terms of how they relate to us. The goods they seek and the skills and virtues by which they create them are part of God's world, and in coming to understand those goods, skills, and virtues, we also understand more of God. At crucial points, theocentric inclusiveness should set the church and its people apart from a world that recruits in order to divide. The church takes up space that helps preserve the shrinking middle ground where people do not already have all the answers. Love embraces genuine difference in faith that there is more to God's creation than the divided society we have created for ourselves.

Elusiveness

From the beginning, Christians have been encouraged to speak up boldly when their faith is challenged, leaving no one in doubt about the witness they bear (Acts 4:13). This has been important in authoritarian states where the church has been persecuted and in closed communities where speaking up for the outsider may result in social ostracism, or worse. Perhaps because the United States has had a long history of relatively free religious expression, the example of the bold witness has a favored place in many of our traditions of Christian formation. The faith that takes up space like a rock, visible and immovable, seems to be the ideal toward which we should be striving.

But in a society divided the way ours is, speaking boldly may be just another way to underscore the divisions. No social or political authority forbids us to speak boldly, and if the energy is directed against the right targets, any clever thing we say will be retweeted, liked, and shared, widely and almost instantaneously.

In those circumstances, a Christian formed by hope might want to be a little hard to pin down. Like unctuousness, the improbable virtue that knows what to say to the lion when your head is in the lion's mouth,* *elusiveness*

---

* See above, pp. 141–42.

is the virtue of not revealing which side you are on when everybody has to be on one side or the other. Elusiveness is especially important for congregations and church organizations. They are under intense pressure just now to be "progressive" or "traditionalist," "evangelical" or "liberal," and whole denominations are dividing along lines that are in turn steadily assimilated to the polarized oppositions that divide the whole society. Boldness may now seem to require standing up and refusing to be separated from those with whom we disagree, but even that kind of boldness runs the risk of dividing "our" openness from "their" conviction that at some point a choice must be made. It may be better to remain seated and listen. As we have seen throughout this book, listening to the Word and to the world is how faith makes a difference in a divided society.

Those who are listening are hard to pin down, because they are not simply asserting their own positions. People find it easy to identify you when you are wearing your T-shirt on your way to the rally. Trying to understand the world from a different point of view requires at least a brief pause in proclaiming our own ideas, and we should not underestimate how difficult that is. Self-interest always exerts a powerful influence on the way we see the world, and the polarized interpretations of events all around us raise anxiety that if we let our guard down, sinister forces are waiting to take advantage of us. Under these conditions, listening to the world is an act of faith. It is not what we know about other people that makes it possible, but what we believe about God as the ultimate reality in whom our conflicts, misperceptions, and self-deceptions are resolved.

Effectiveness

Strange times create new virtues. Churches and Christians who have learned inclusiveness and elusiveness devote less time to virtue signaling and consumer identities. They can turn their attention to the human goods they know how to create, and they are free to build new connections to other people and institutions, so that the goods they create are more widely shared and more securely built into the structures of society. Widely shared goods that involve more and more people in the circles of responsibility that maintain them leave less space, in turn, for the structures of racism, caste, and economic domination. At least that is how listening to the world is supposed to work.

In a divided society, however, those who want to be effective in bringing penultimate goods into being and making them available learn quickly not to make too much of the inclusiveness of their goals. To announce that you are starting a new community organization to fight racism or setting up a mentoring program to help single mothers make use of public assistance programs invites suspicion that you have been reading up on socialism or critical race theory. Shortly, you may hear of alternative programs being devised to support local entrepreneurship and family financial independence. There may be little difference, at bottom, between the details of the different programs, but the shrinking moral vocabulary of our public life often means that the available terms in which to make an argument for the good you want are already polarized.

In these circumstances, as we have seen, the best argument for a good is actually to create it.* If the goal is to sustain polarized politics by giving voice to one side or the other, there are plenty of arguments available, T-shirts to be handed out, and virtues to be signaled. But if we seek goods that have their own penultimate significance in a world where God is the ultimate reality, living in a divided society turns our attention to *effectiveness*. Talk helps to locate you at one or the other of the poles. People are more likely to join you if you are getting something done, making changes at a local level where problems and solutions can speak for themselves.

Effectiveness in bringing concrete goods into being for real people who need them requires attention to skills and virtues, rather than slogans and party labels. It also sends you in search of other people who have those same skills and virtues, and no doubt some new ones that you did not think of at first, so that the good you can create gets connected to other goods in ways that ensure its future. As a result, you may find that being effective makes you inclusive and elusive, too. Focusing on concrete goods and goals is apt to draw a more interesting mix of people than starting with a slogan, and the resulting group may be hard to pin down in a world that is used to only two options.

Change

Effective work by people in inclusive groups that elude the labels that a divided society wants to pin on them fits the ancient understanding of politics discussed earlier in this

---

* See above, p. 125.

book.* Politics, as Aristotle described it, involves people creating the goods they need to live together, acquiring the skills and virtues they need to do this, and thus also securing a good life for themselves. That we might want to expand on Aristotle's list of skills and virtues and extend the possibility of a good life to more people than he considered only enlarges the importance of this kind of politics, widely shared among people to whom Christians need to listen when they are listening to the world.

Whether this politics of concrete goods shared by people who have the virtues they need to maintain them can change the polarized politics that dominates our news media, divides our society, and occupies the attention of the people we call "politicians" is a difficult question. From the first pages of this book, what we have seen is that behind the rhetoric of crisis that shapes immediate reactions to events, polarization has become a remarkably stable way of organizing political life at a national level. Both sides benefit from having an easy target to blame for problems that we all share, and an attempt to challenge polarization itself is easily assigned to one pole or the other, so that it becomes part of the problem it meant to challenge. Any church that speaks up against polarization will almost certainly be understood to speak for one side and against the other, becoming another one of the adaptations to a divided society that already obscure what is distinctive about the Word the church proclaims. The question, then, is whether the church and its work of formation simply takes up space until something else happens, or whether taking up space by listening to the

* See above, p. 120.

Word, to the world, and to those who are not heard might itself lead to significant changes.

One possibility suggested by this discussion of effectiveness, elusiveness, and inclusiveness is that local efforts devoted to concrete goods become demonstration projects for a politics that does not depend on consumer identities, virtue signaling, or exaggerated claims about the ultimate significance of penultimate choices. Churches are in a good position to bring these projects to wider attention, because what they do often involves recognized human needs and builds on collaboration with other groups. In addition, churches have a network of connections, locally and globally, to create programs that reach across the predictable divides between communities, classes, and interests. But the church's work of formation is not confined to mission projects. It reaches beyond its own institutional limits to include the ways that Christians live their whole lives, as they find opportunities to demonstrate effectiveness in surprising new ways, reach out to include new people, and defy polarized expectations about who will be able to work together.

Through all of this, the church bears witness to the ultimate unity of all things in God that is the ground of all of these proximate demonstrations of human unity. At this point in our history, however, it is important to remember that penultimate goods have their own importance and integrity. We can discuss them with one another as limited goods that meet shared needs, without requiring theological agreement on their ultimate meaning and without supplying a political program that ties them all together in one package. As we come to understand the goods for which we are responsible and learn to talk about them with one another, the first important task is to secure these penultimate goods themselves. But we might also begin to re-create a vocabulary for the public discourse that has largely disappeared. We need terms that belong to no party and have no enemies. If life, health, choice, freedom, inquiry, and identity cannot provide the vocabulary, we will have to find it among the miscellaneous needs that we meet in concrete ways as we listen to the world. Food packages might do, and safe places to sleep. A book to read, and some of those skills at baking, farming, and making that have tended to pass beneath the notice of ethics professors, along with those skills in the lab, clinic, and accounting office that we know we all depend on. Something interesting to see or hear when the work is done, and maybe a story at bedtime. For the moment, at least, the more ordinary these concrete goods we talk about are, the better.

At some point, it may even be possible to point out to our political leaders that government itself is a penultimate good that allows us, within the limits of human finitude, to do justice to one another and to secure the penultimate goods which we create together. If we can demonstrate how to be effective, elusive, and inclusive in creating other penultimate goods, perhaps we can do it for government, too. But that will depend on keeping those political goals appropriately concrete and limited. For that, we will need a church that bears witness to the unity of the ultimate and takes up space by forming people who know how to listen to the Word, to the world, and to one another.

Questions for Reflection and Discussion

Chapter 1: Polarization

1. Where do you experience the divisions in our society in your own life? Does polarization affect relationships in your workplace? Your family? Your church?

2. How do you tell the difference between normal disagreements and polarization that hardens into permanent divisions? What are the signs in your own experience that disagreements are becoming polarized?

3. Instead of polarization, philosophers and theologians suggest that democracy depends on "reasonable pluralism," where people find "proximate solutions for insoluble problems" (see above, p. 7). Do you see this ideal at work in our public life today? Is "reasonable pluralism" compatible with Christian commitment?

4. How have the places where you work, worship, and live adapted to polarization? Has a divided society become our normal way of life?

5. When do you think our present divisions began? Were there particular events that brought them into being, or is polarization a gradual development from many different

trends? How might someone who is older or younger than yourself have experienced these changes differently?

Chapter 2: The Church in a Polarized Society

1. Dietrich Bonhoeffer insisted that the church of Jesus Christ must "take up space" in the world. What does that idea mean to you?

2. Where do you see the church and Christians "taking up space" in our society today? How can we tell the difference between "taking up space" that demonstrates our faith and a role that simply contributes to the divisions that have been drawn by others?

3. What are the "things before the last" that are important to Christian life today? How can we relate "penultimate" goods to our faith commitments without shortchanging one or the other?

4. What are the penultimate goods that are most important in your life? In the life of contemporary society? What are the most important ways that you are involved in creating and maintaining these goods?

5. What are the specific ways that your congregation "takes up space" in the local community and the wider world? What are the concrete goods that are most important to that work?

Chapter 3: Listening to the Word

1. The theologian H. Richard Niebuhr said that "God is acting in all actions upon you." Do you agree with that?

How would your view of the world be different if you took that idea seriously?

2. Has Christianity become a kind of "consumer identity" that encourages Christians to set themselves apart from others? How does this relate to the other identities that are available in a divided society?

3. How does your church provide "formation" in the Christian life? Can the church provide a distinctive identity without withdrawing from a divided society?

4. The theological virtues of faith, hope, and love have long been central to Christian formation. How does our understanding of them need to change for the time in which we now live? Is there one of these theological virtues that is particularly important for our time? What key things about faith, hope, and love remain constant through these changes?

Chapter 4: Listening to the World

1. How would you describe your own "circle of responsibility" (see above, p. 103)? What activities and organizations are central to it? How does it connect you to other people and their circles of responsibility? How has your circle of responsibility changed over time?

2. What are the most important concrete goods that you create and maintain through these responsibilities?

3. How does your circle of responsibility shape you as a person? What are the distinctive virtues that you need to develop to meet your responsibilities?

4. Does your circle of responsibility provide opportunities to discuss the goods and virtues that you create and main-

tain there? Are there ways that you could encourage more of these discussions, and would it be helpful if you did?

5.   How does your church encourage or discourage listening to the world?

Chapter 5: Listening to Those Who Are Not Heard

1.   Who are the people you encounter in daily life whom you do not hear? Why are they not heard?

2.   Where are you not heard? How would being heard help you create and maintain the goods for which you are responsible? What skills and virtues would you need to expand your circle of responsibility in this way?

3.   What skills and virtues are undervalued in your circle of responsibility? What would change if you gave more attention to these things? Where could you find people with these skills and virtues, and how could you develop them in yourself and others?

4.   What are the boundaries and barriers that keep people from listening to one another, even when they live in close proximity? How can your congregation and other churches work together to remove those barriers?

5.   What ways can you see to make a more effective case for the penultimate goods that are important in your circle of responsibility?

Index